MYTHOLOGY GRA

PERSEPHONE
AND THE UNDERWORLD

A MODERN GRAPHIC GREEK MYTH

BY JESSICA GUNDERSON
ILLUSTRATED BY JESSI ZABARSKY
COVER BY LE NHAT VU

CAPSTONE PRESS
a capstone imprint

Published by Capstone Press, an imprint of Capstone
1710 Roe Crest Drive, North Mankato, Minnesota 56003
capstonepub.com

Library of Congress Cataloging-in-Publication Data is available
on the Library of Congress website.

ISBN: 9781669050858 (hardcover)
ISBN: 9781669050803 (paperback)
ISBN: 9781669050810 (ebook PDF)

Summary: Hades, god of the Underworld, has his eyes on a potential bride—
Persephone. When he forces her to live with him in the Underworld, Persephone's
mother, the goddess of nature, is not happy. Soon, Earth falls into ruin. In order to
set things right, the Greek gods and goddesses must make a compromise. Learn
Persephone's story in this modern, graphic retelling of a classic Greek myth.

Editorial Credits
Editor: Alison Deering; Designer: Jaime Willems;
Production Specialist: Whitney Schaefer

All internet sites appearing in back matter were available and accurate when
this book was sent to press.

Printed and bound in the USA.   PO#5425

TABLE OF CONTENTS

CHAPTER 1

NATURE GIRL

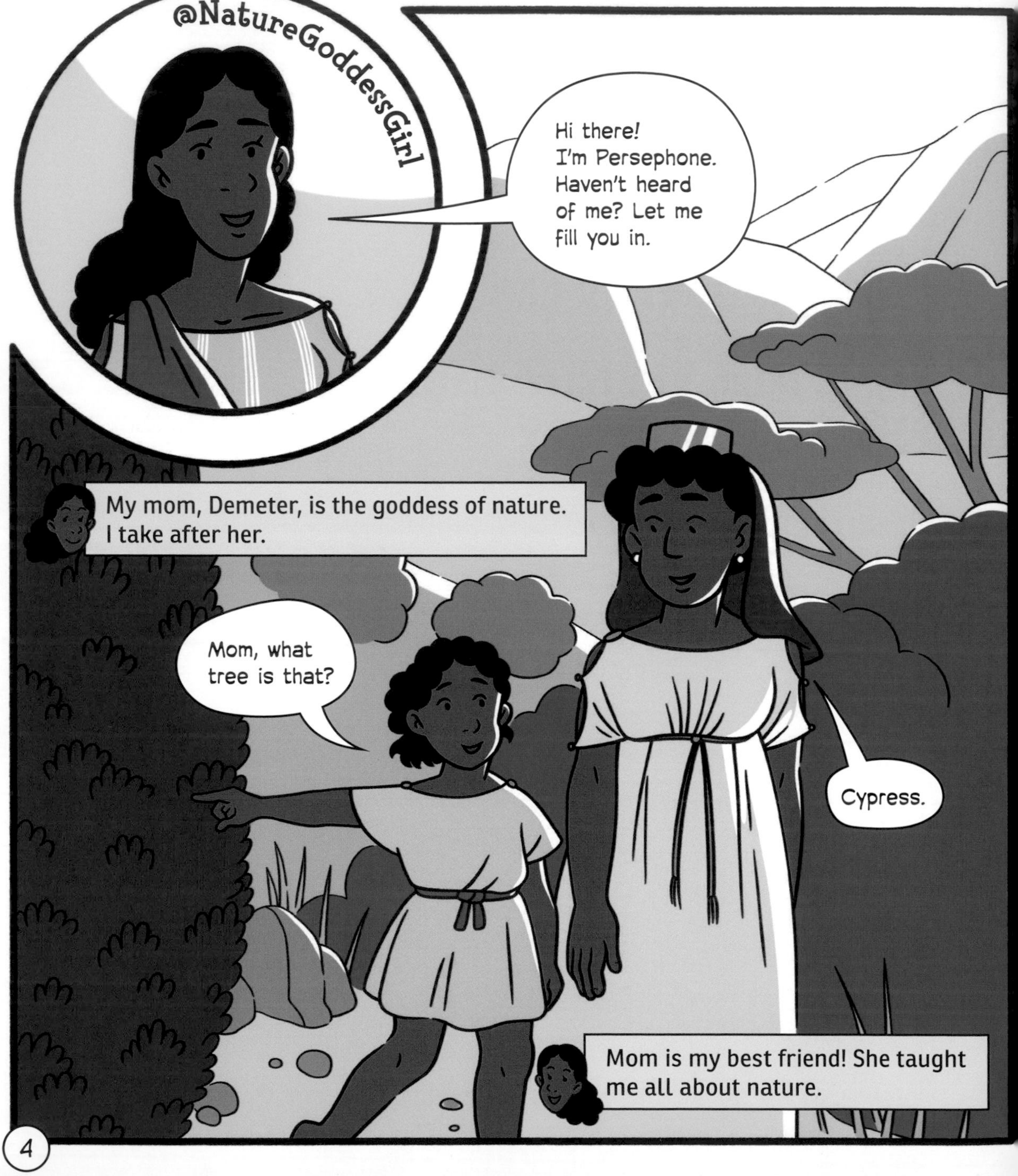

@NatureGoddessGirl
Hi there! I'm Persephone. Haven't heard of me? Let me fill you in.
My mom, Demeter, is the goddess of nature. I take after her.
Mom, what tree is that?
Cypress.
Mom is my best friend! She taught me all about nature.

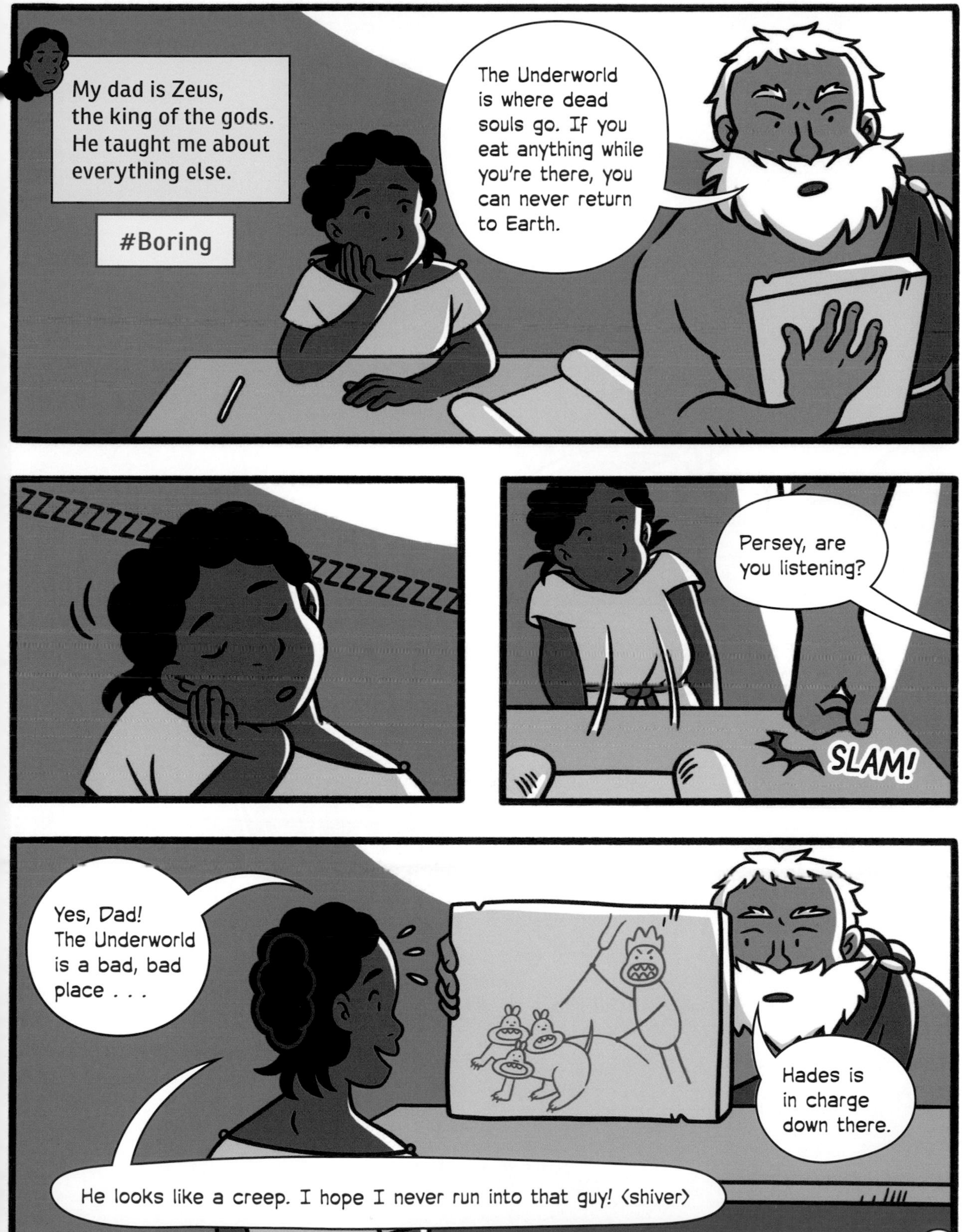
My dad is Zeus, the king of the gods. He taught me about everything else.
#Boring
The Underworld is where dead souls go. If you eat anything while you're there, you can never return to Earth.
ZZZZZZZZZZ
ZZZZZZZZZZ
Persey, are you listening?
SLAM!
Yes, Dad! The Underworld is a bad, bad place . . .
Hades is in charge down there.
He looks like a creep. I hope I never run into that guy! <shiver>

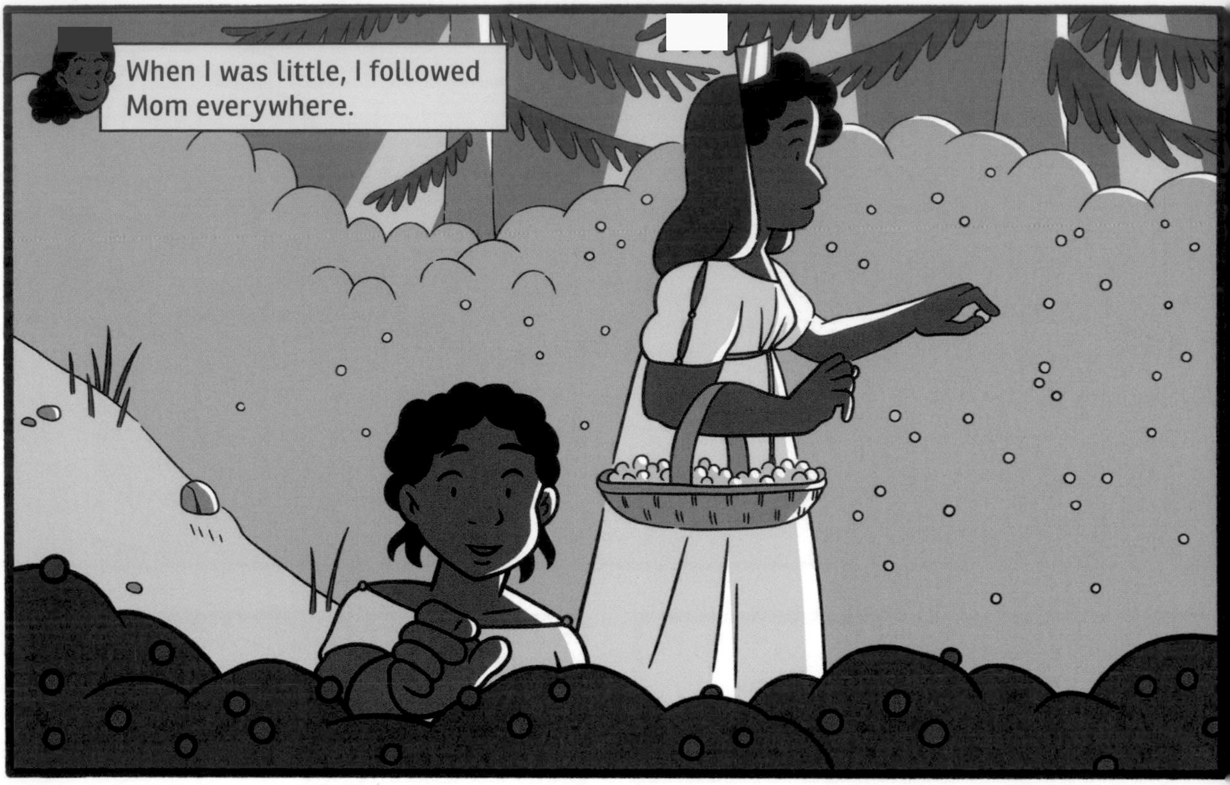
When I was little, I followed Mom everywhere.

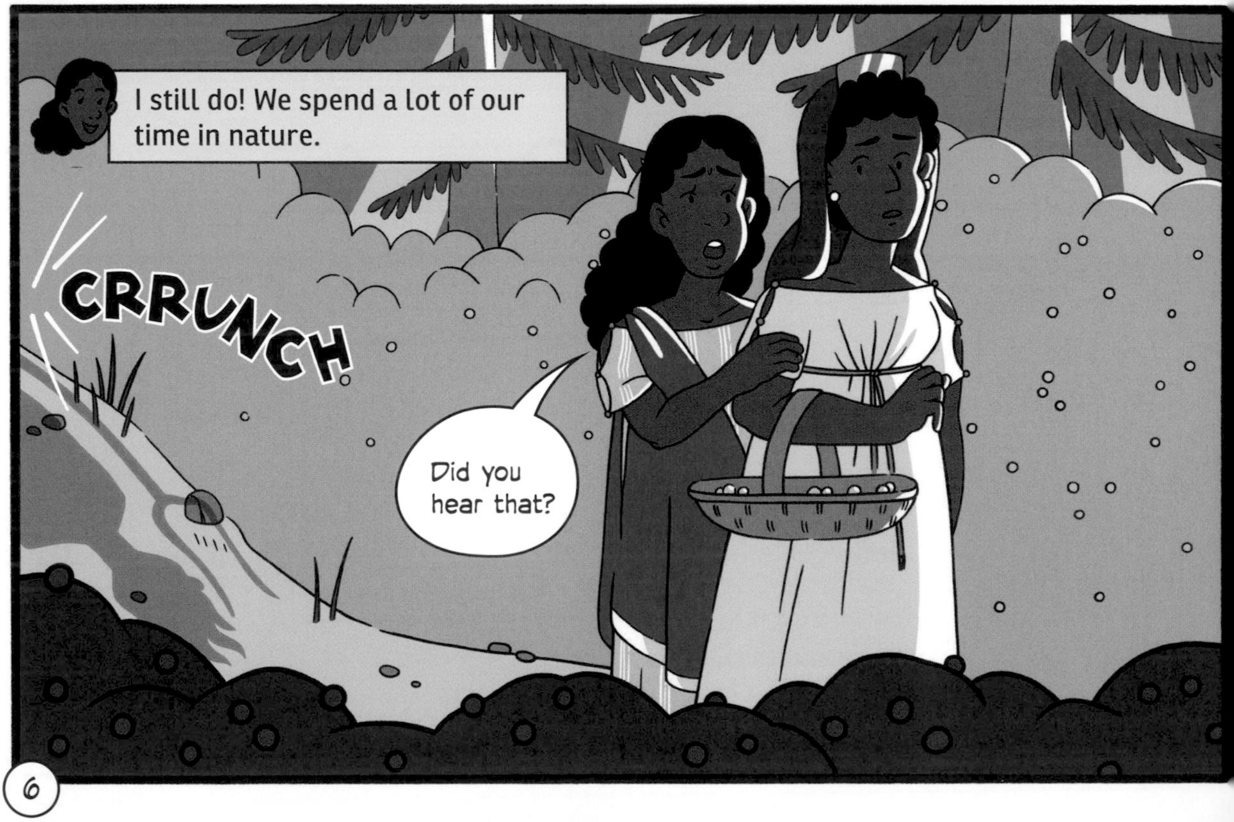
I still do! We spend a lot of our time in nature.
CRRUNCH
Did you hear that?

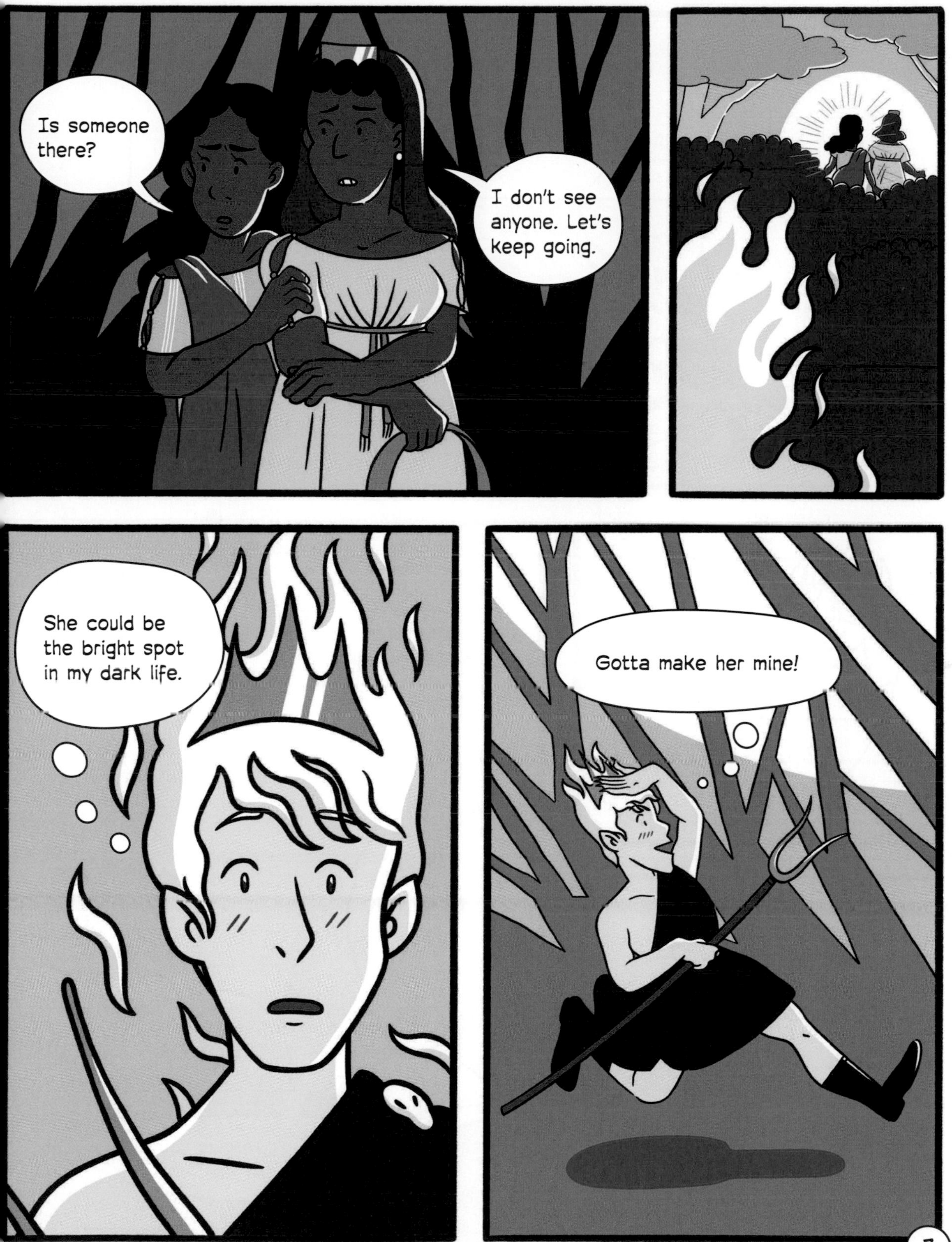
Is someone there?
I don't see anyone. Let's keep going.
She could be the bright spot in my dark life.
Gotta make her mine!

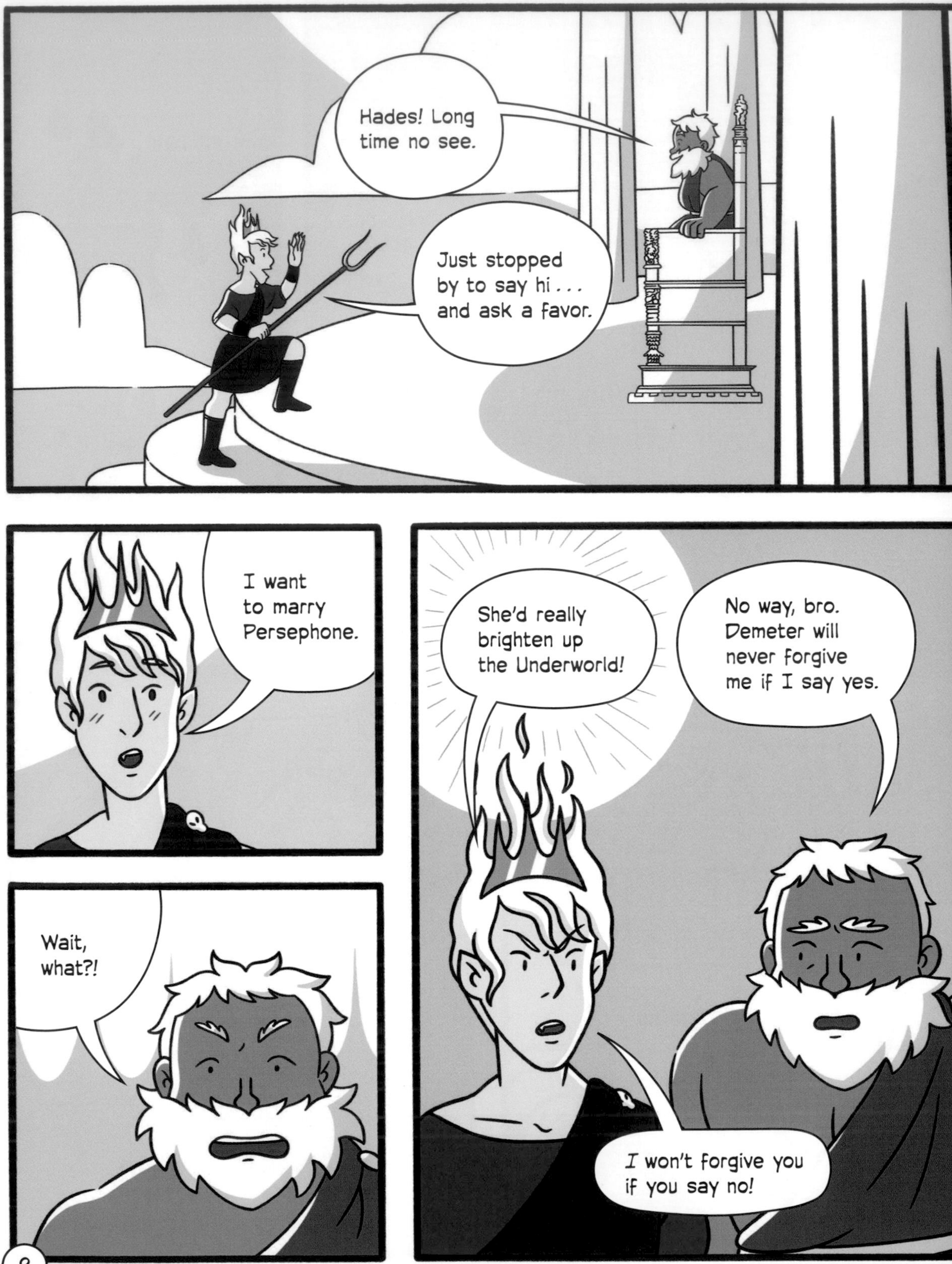
Hades! Long time no see.
Just stopped by to say hi . . . and ask a favor.
I want to marry Persephone.
Wait, what?!
She'd really brighten up the Underworld!
No way, bro. Demeter will never forgive me if I say yes.
I won't forgive you if you say no!

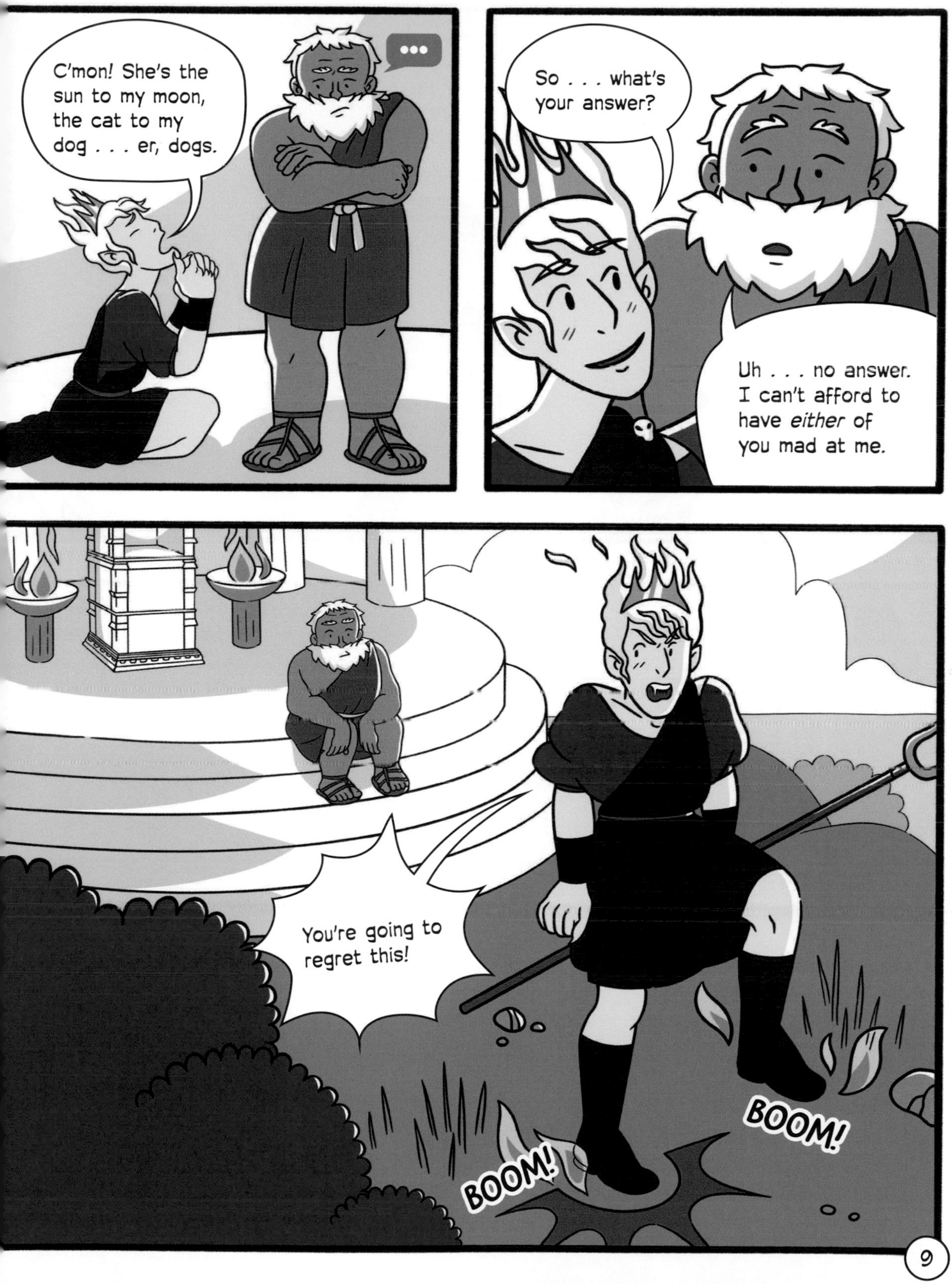
C'mon! She's the sun to my moon, the cat to my dog . . . er, dogs.
So . . . what's your answer?
Uh . . . no answer. I can't afford to have *either* of you mad at me.
You're going to regret this!
BOOM!
BOOM!

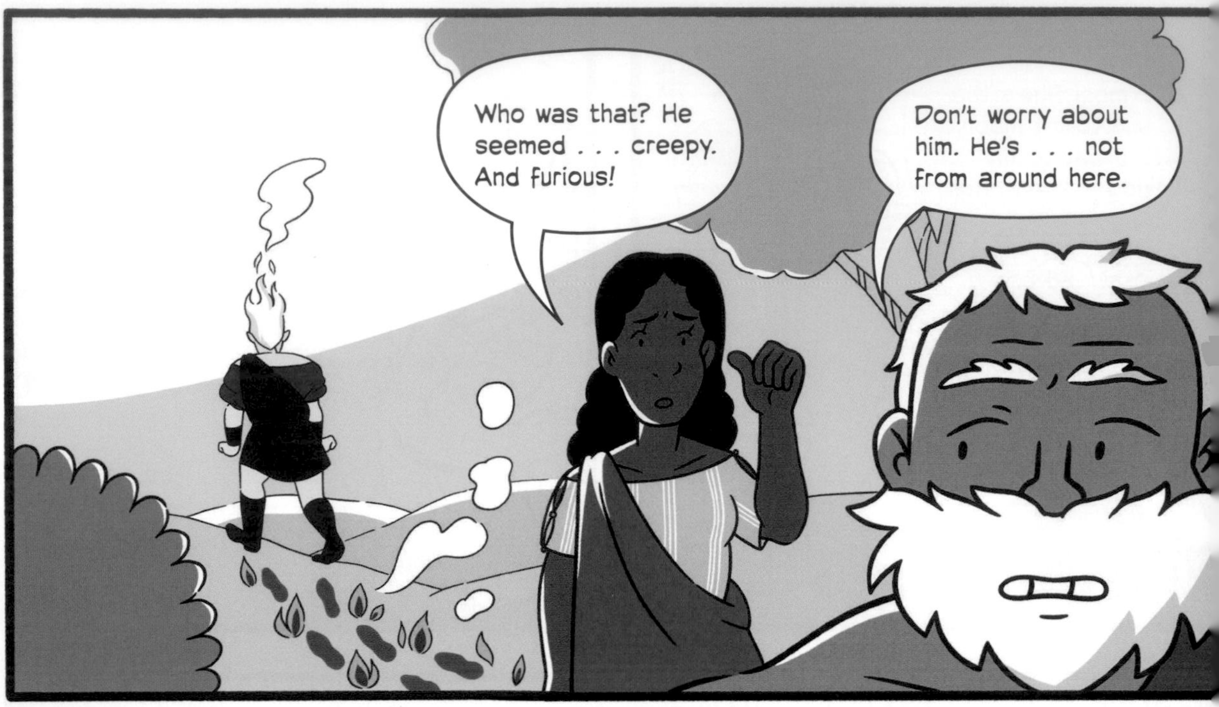
Who was that? He seemed . . . creepy. And furious!
Don't worry about him. He's . . . not from around here.

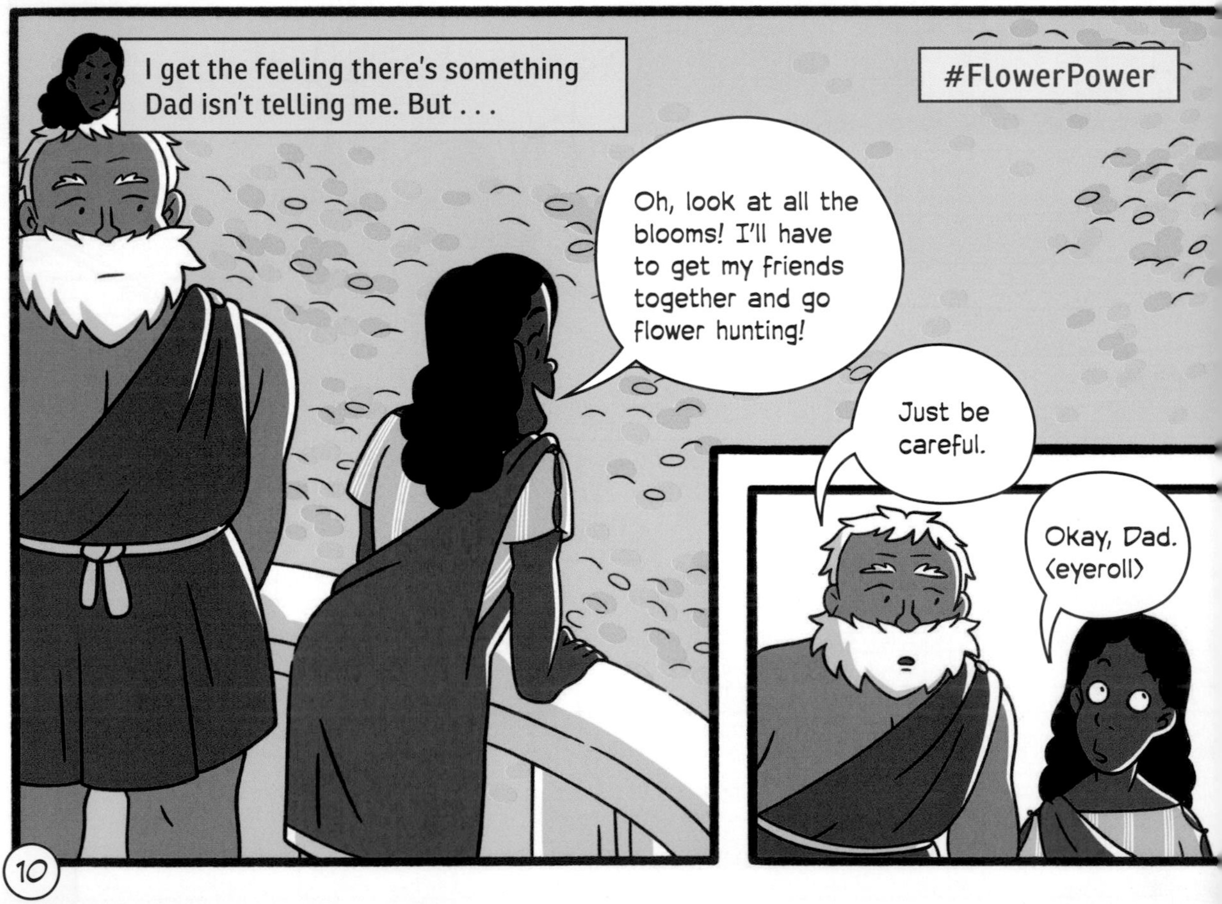
I get the feeling there's something Dad isn't telling me. But . . .
#FlowerPower
Oh, look at all the blooms! I'll have to get my friends together and go flower hunting!
Just be careful.
Okay, Dad. <eyeroll>

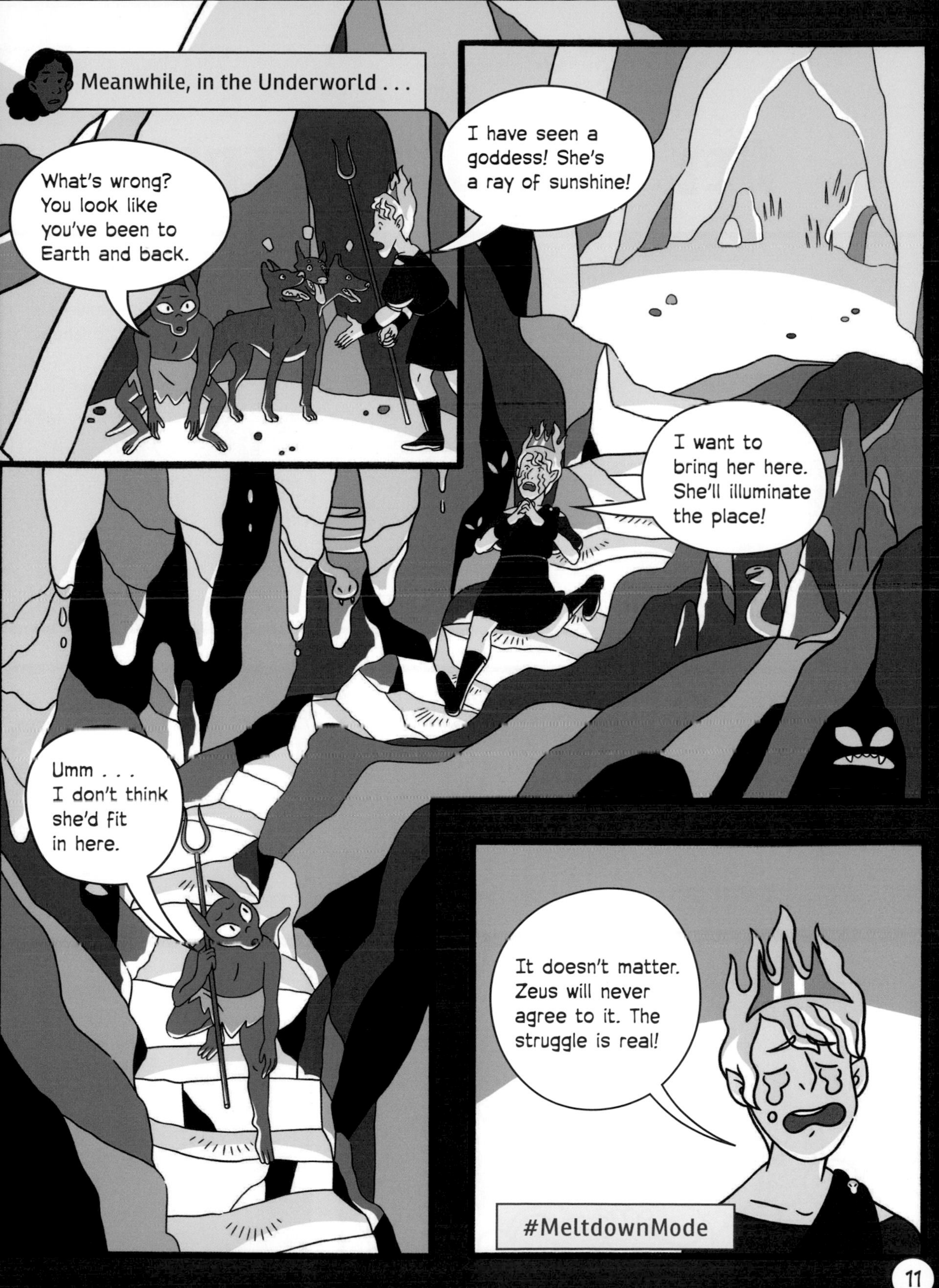
Meanwhile, in the Underworld . . .
What's wrong? You look like you've been to Earth and back.
I have seen a goddess! She's a ray of sunshine!
I want to bring her here. She'll illuminate the place!
Umm . . . I don't think she'd fit in here.
It doesn't matter. Zeus will never agree to it. The struggle is real!
#MeltdownMode

CHAPTER 2

GET ME OUTTA HERE!

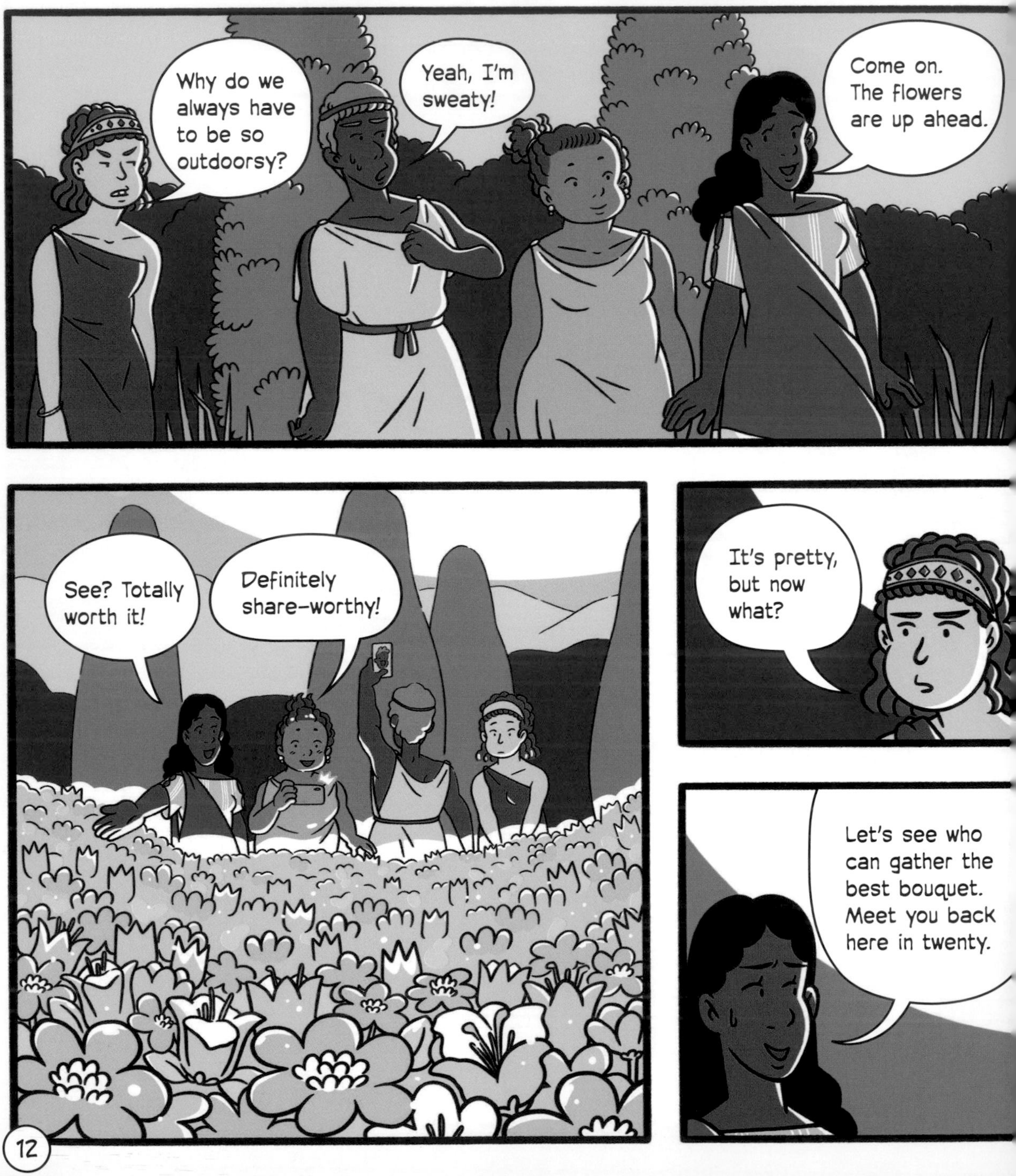

Why do we always have to be so outdoorsy?
Yeah, I'm sweaty!
Come on. The flowers are up ahead.
See? Totally worth it!
Definitely share-worthy!
It's pretty, but now what?
Let's see who can gather the best bouquet. Meet you back here in twenty.

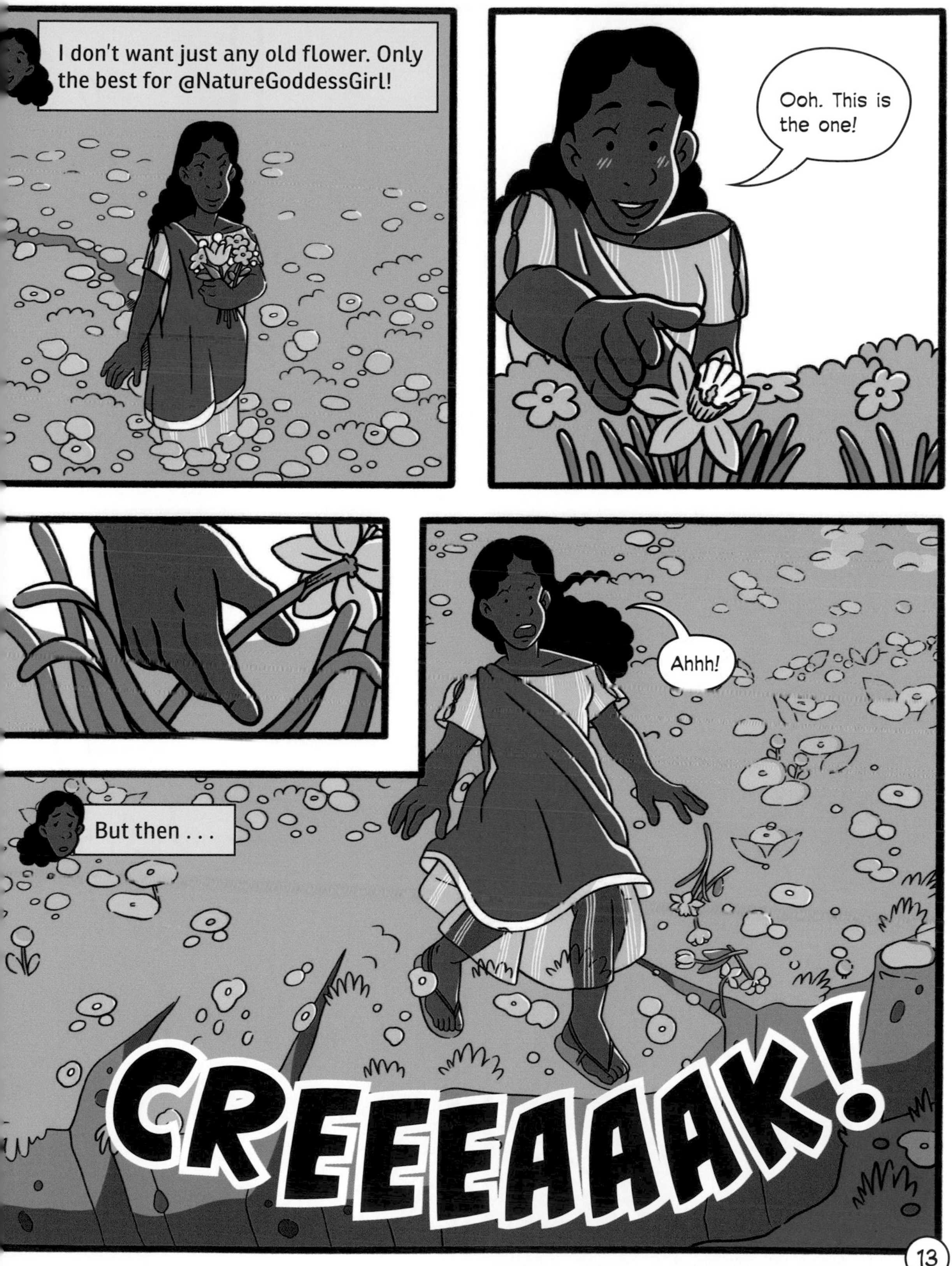
I don't want just any old flower. Only the best for @NatureGoddessGirl!
Ooh. This is the one!
Ahhh!
But then . . .
CREEEAAAK!

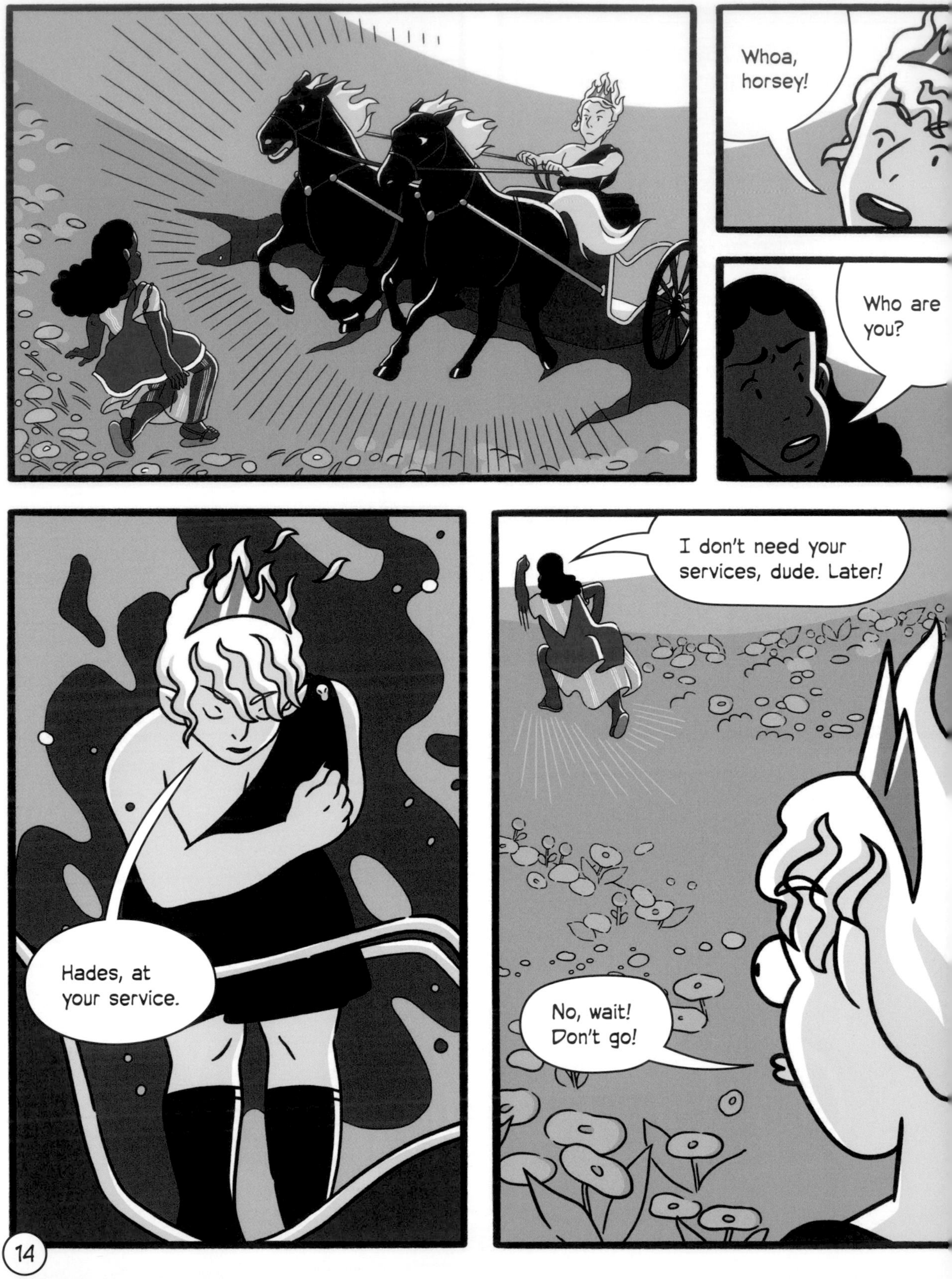
Whoa, horsey!
Who are you?
Hades, at your service.
I don't need your services, dude. Later!
No, wait! Don't go!

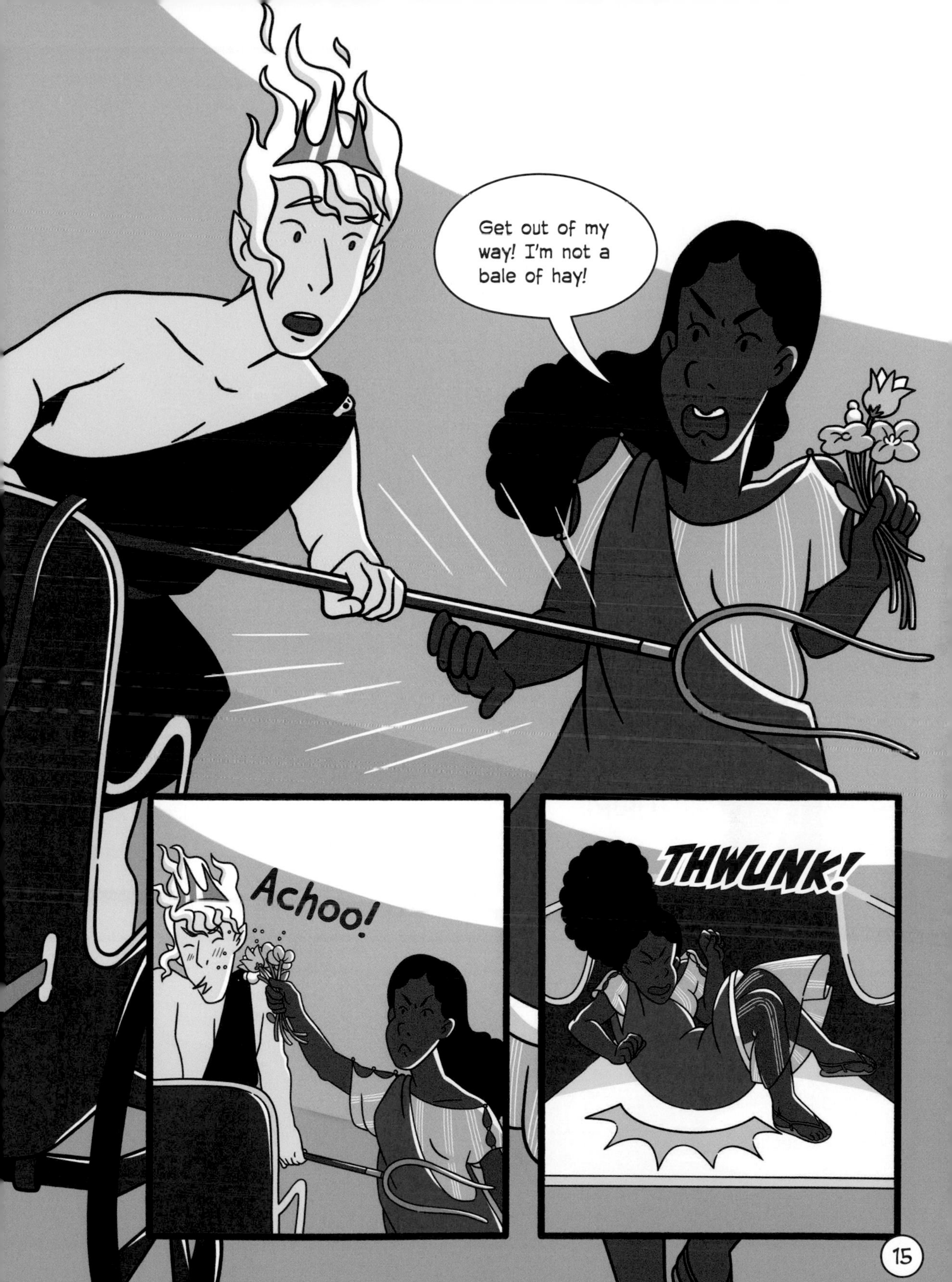
Get out of my way! I'm not a bale of hay!
Achoo!
THWUNK!

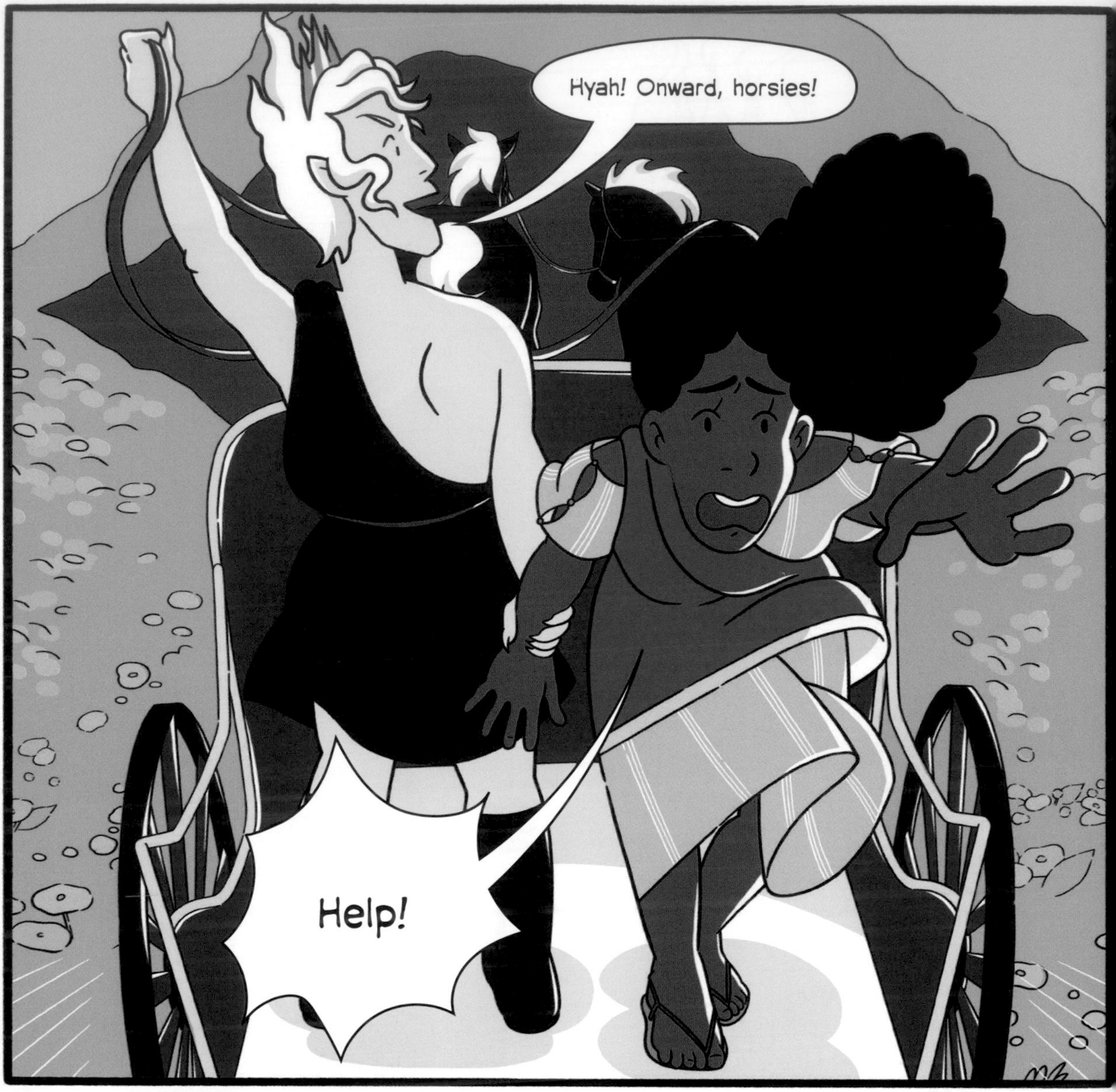
Hyah! Onward, horsies!
Help!

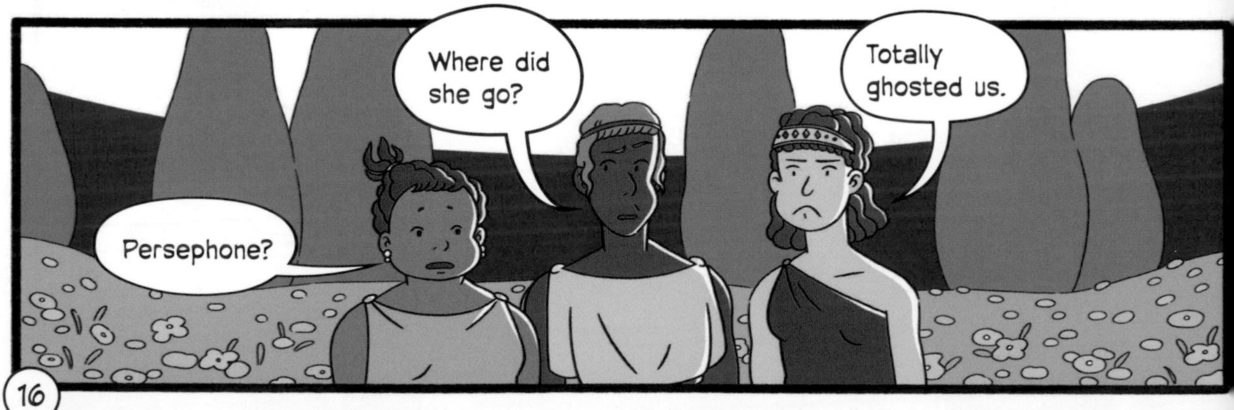
Persephone?
Where did she go?
Totally ghosted us.

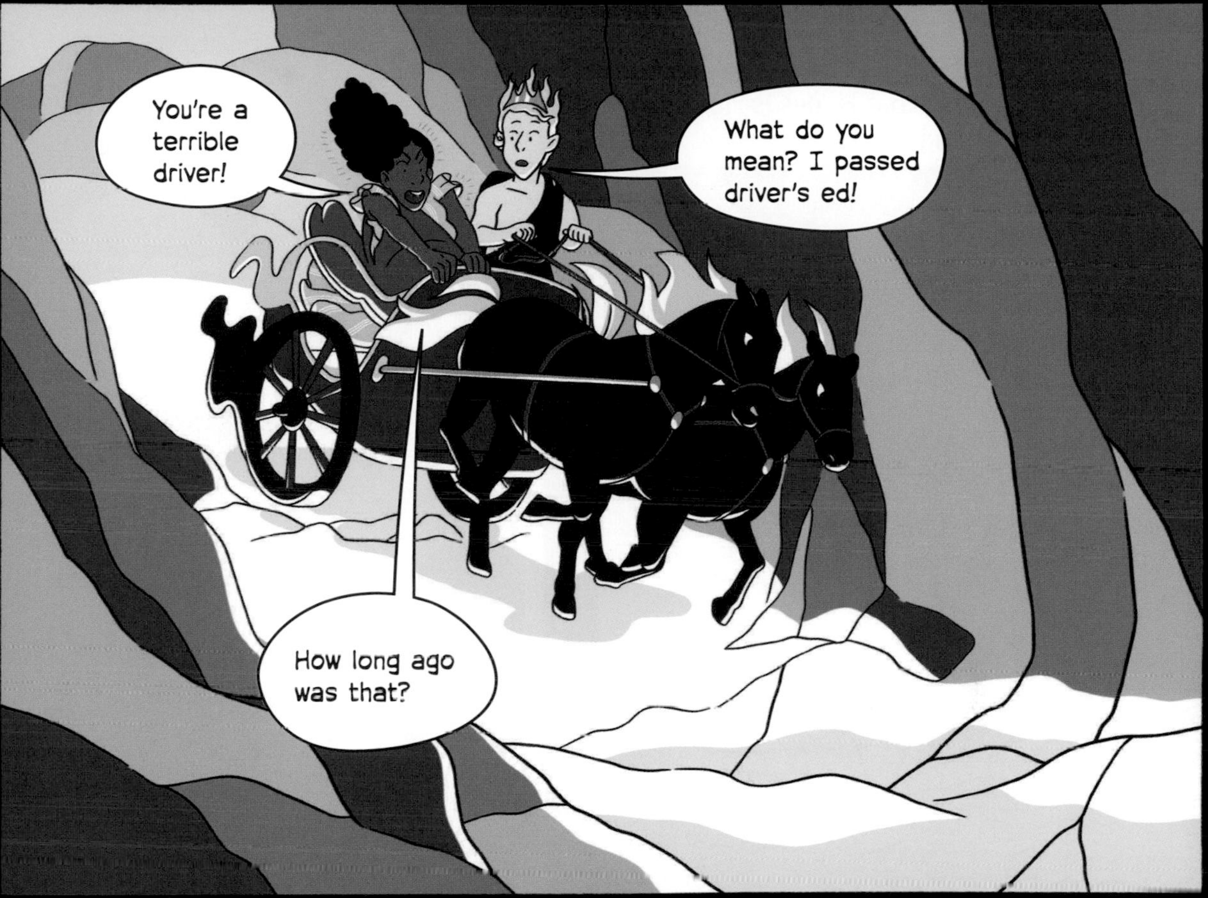
You're a terrible driver!
What do you mean? I passed driver's ed!
How long ago was that?

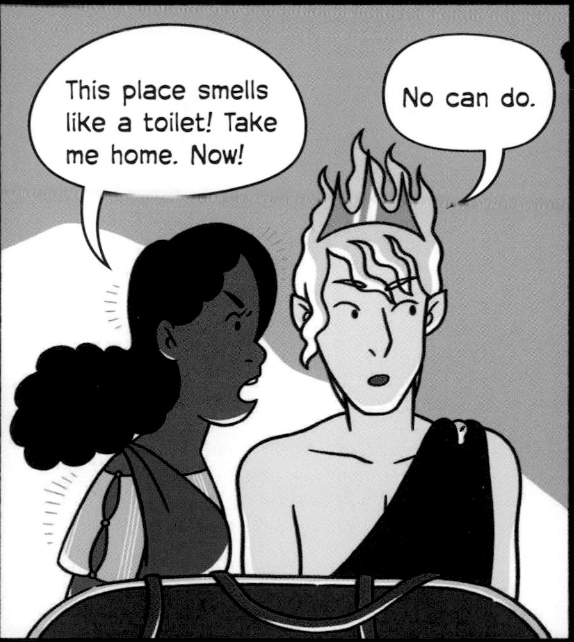
This place smells like a toilet! Take me home. Now!
No can do.

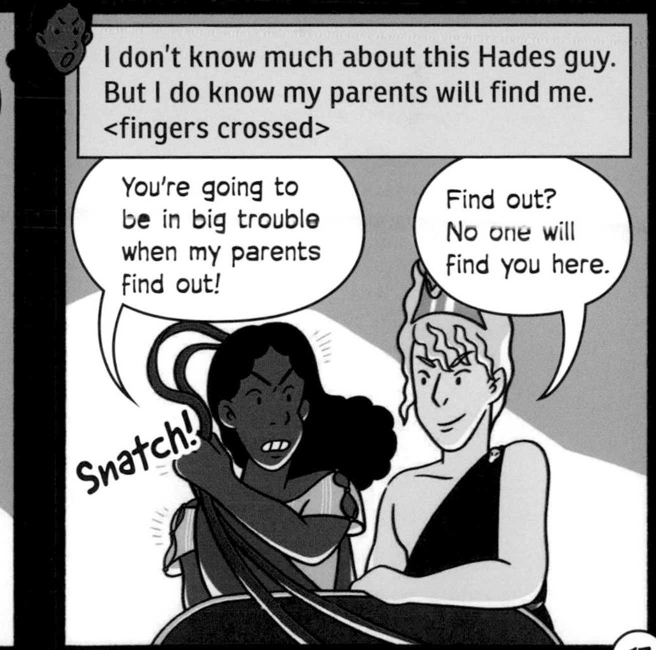
I don't know much about this Hades guy. But I do know my parents will find me. <fingers crossed>
You're going to be in big trouble when my parents find out!
Find out? No one will find you here.
Snatch!

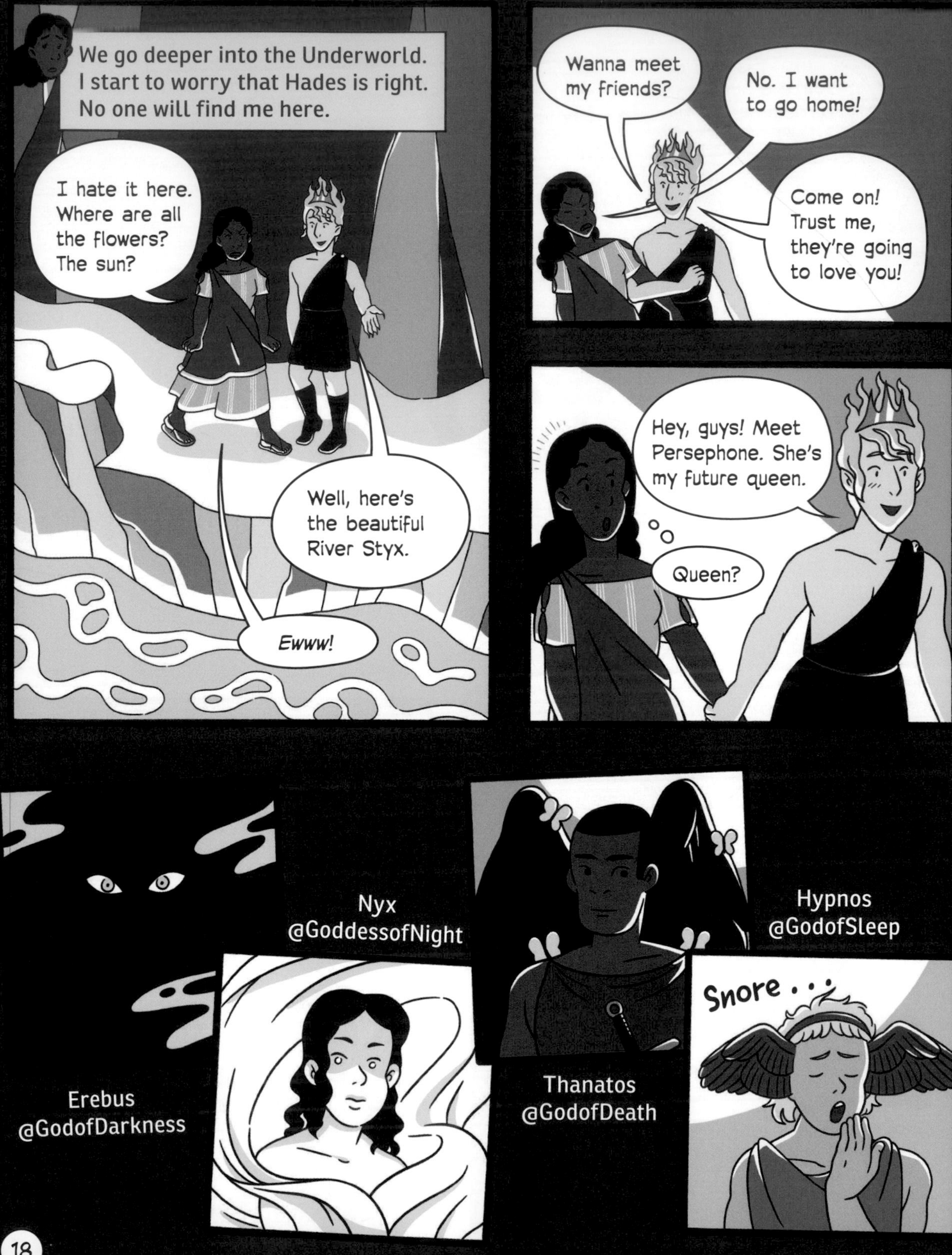
We go deeper into the Underworld. I start to worry that Hades is right. No one will find me here.
I hate it here. Where are all the flowers? The sun?
Well, here's the beautiful River Styx.
Ewww!
Wanna meet my friends?
No. I want to go home!
Come on! Trust me, they're going to love you!
Hey, guys! Meet Persephone. She's my future queen.
Queen?
Erebus @GodofDarkness
Nyx @GoddessofNight
Thanatos @GodofDeath
Hypnos @GodofSleep
Snore . . .

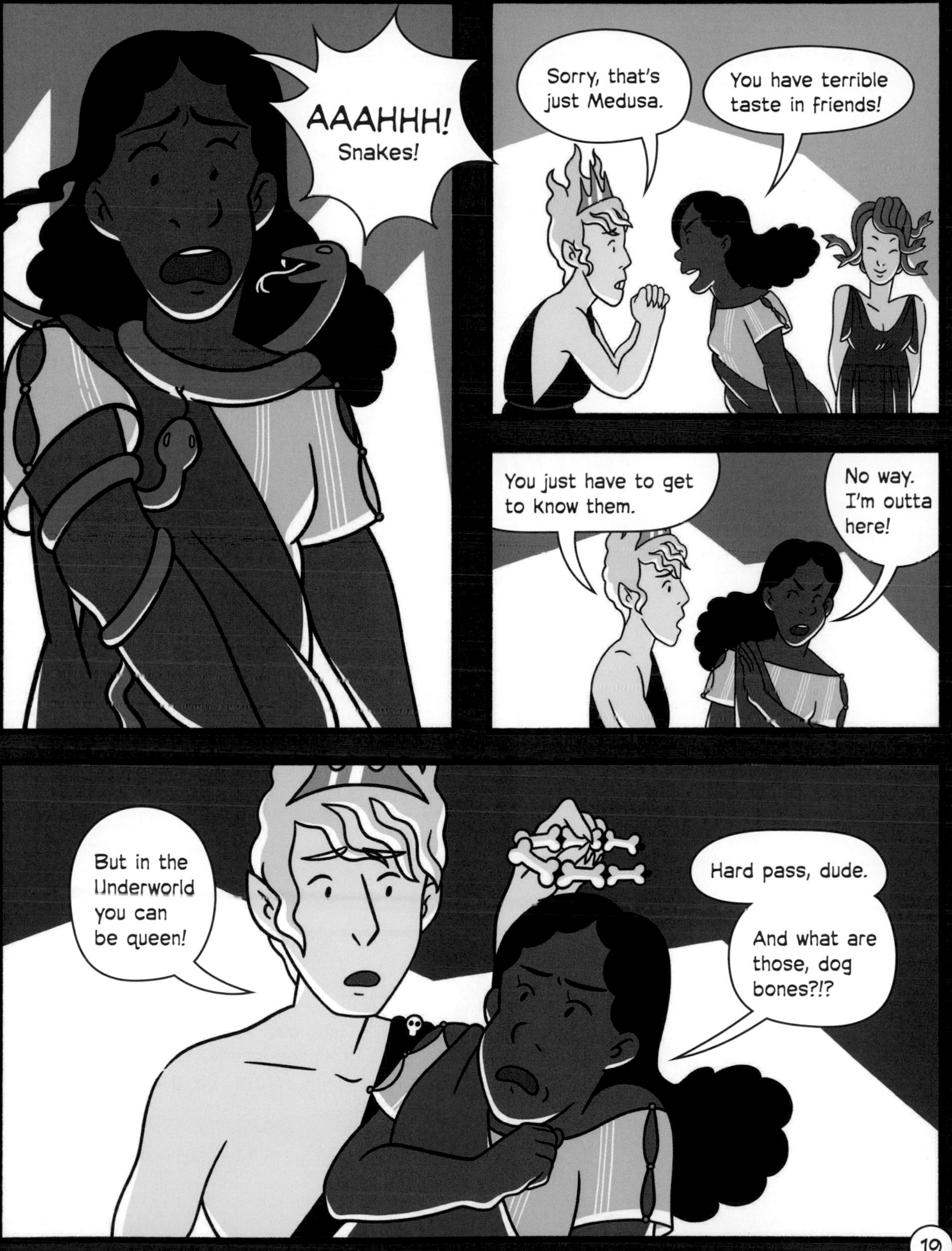
AAAHHH! Snakes!
Sorry, that's just Medusa.
You have terrible taste in friends!
You just have to get to know them.
No way. I'm outta here!
But in the Underworld you can be queen!
Hard pass, dude.
And what are those, dog bones?!?

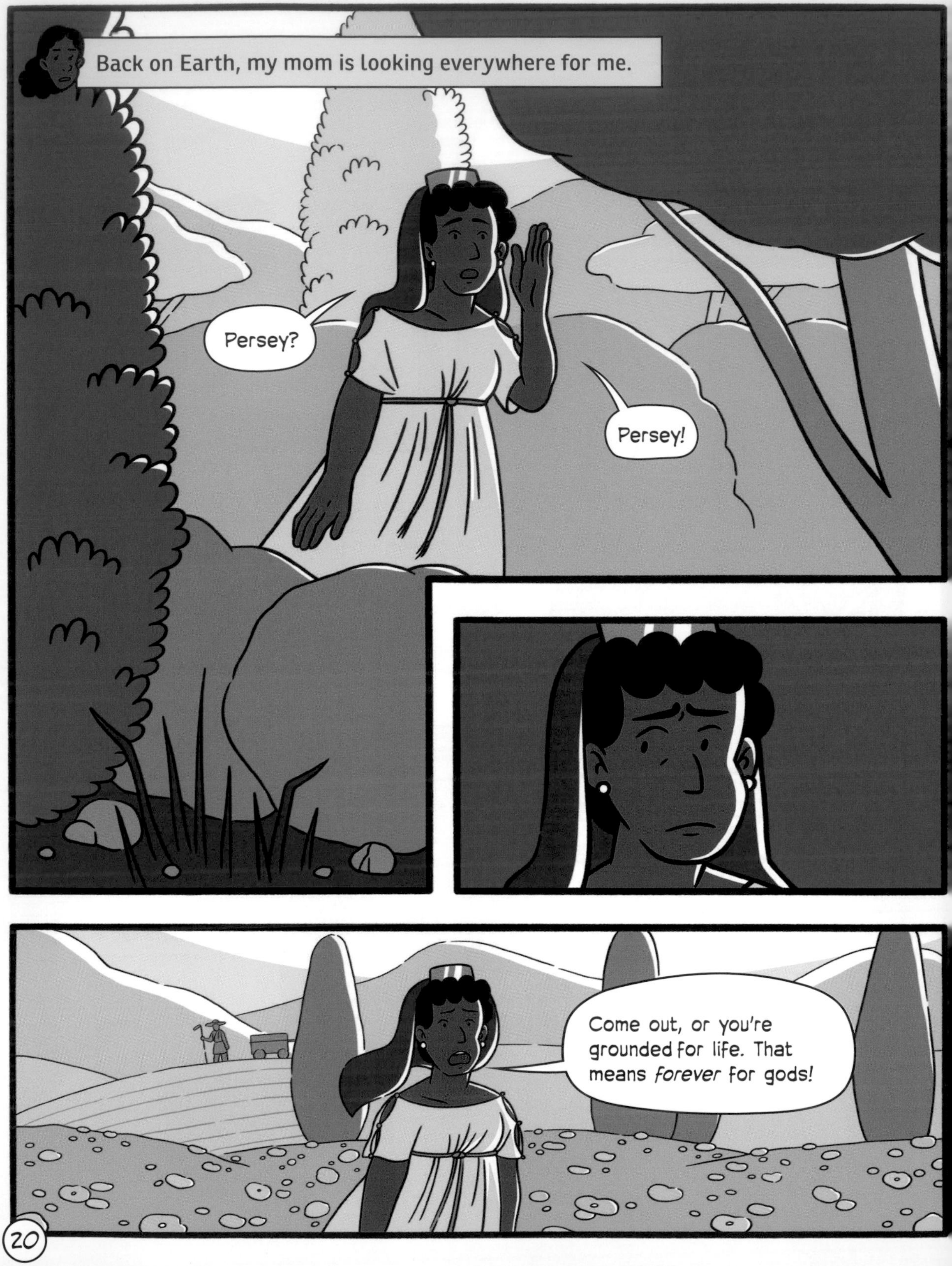
Back on Earth, my mom is looking everywhere for me.
Persey?
Persey!
Come out, or you're grounded for life. That means *forever* for gods!

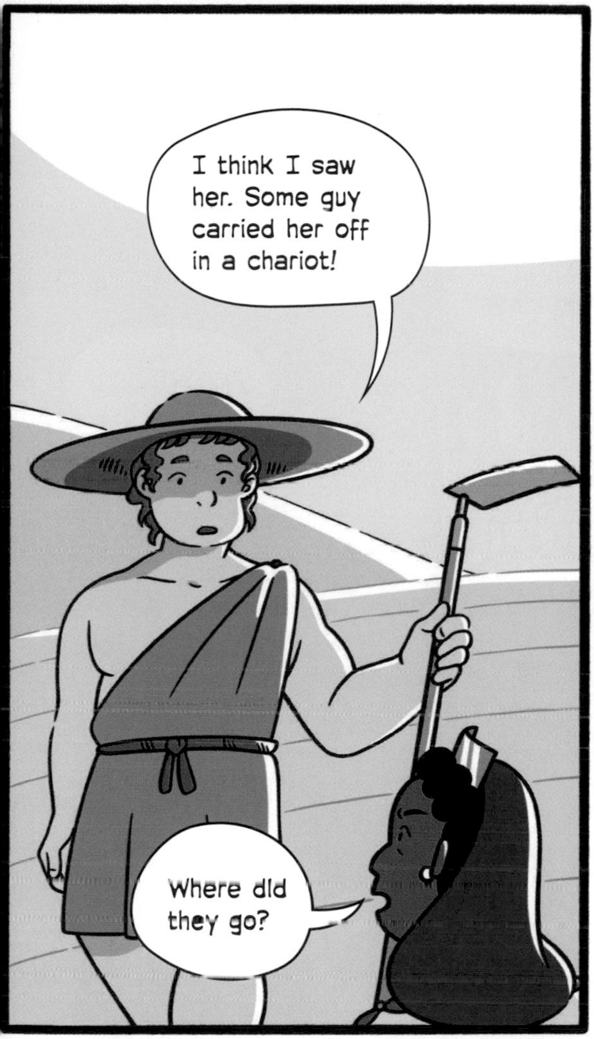
I think I saw her. Some guy carried her off in a chariot!
Where did they go?

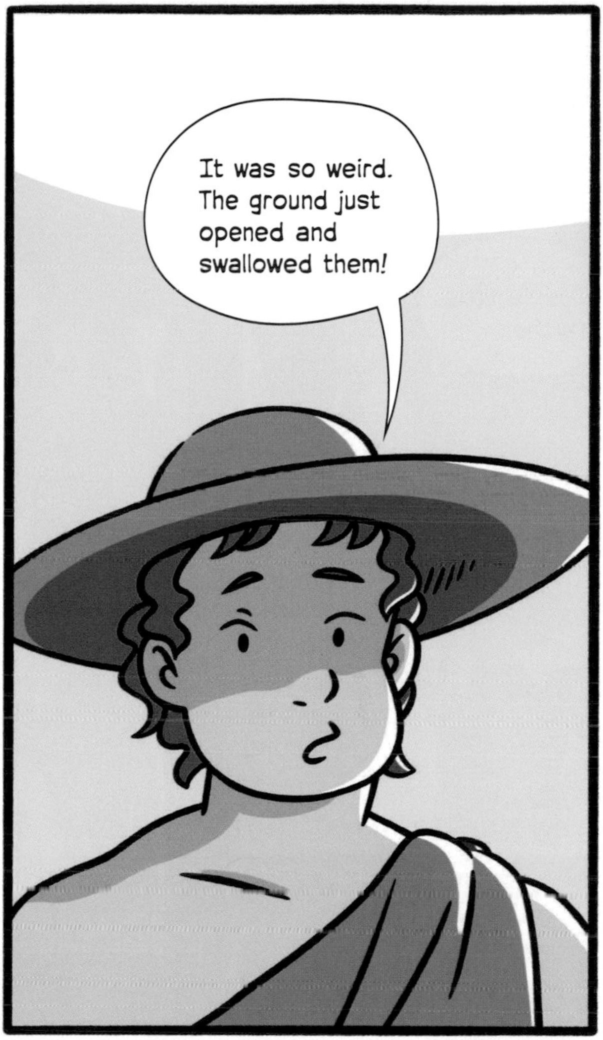
It was so weird. The ground just opened and swallowed them!

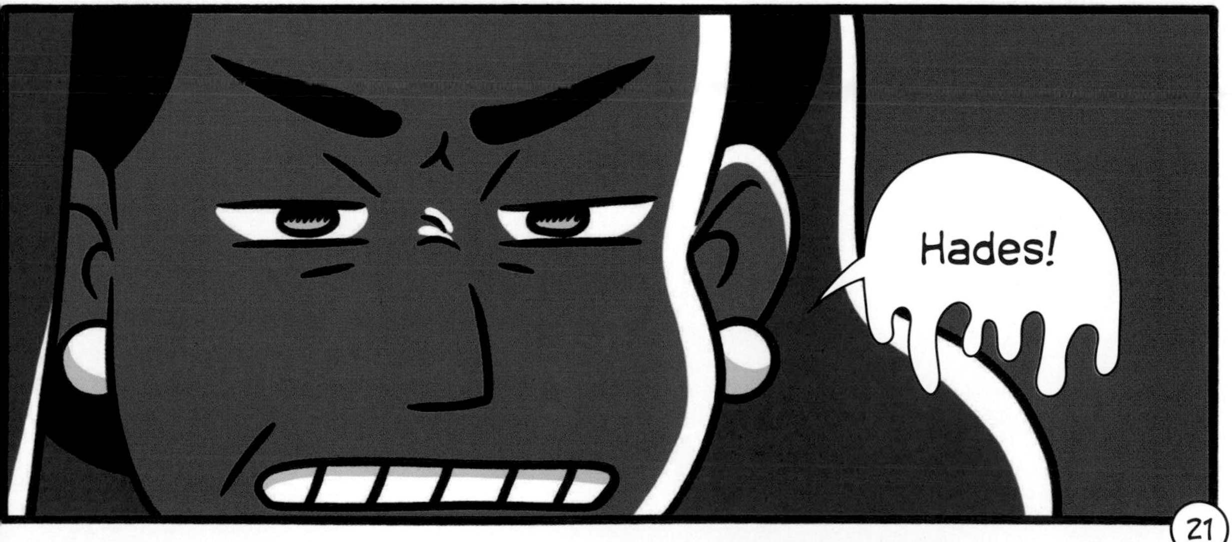
Hades!

CHAPTER 3

THE QUEEN'S CAVE

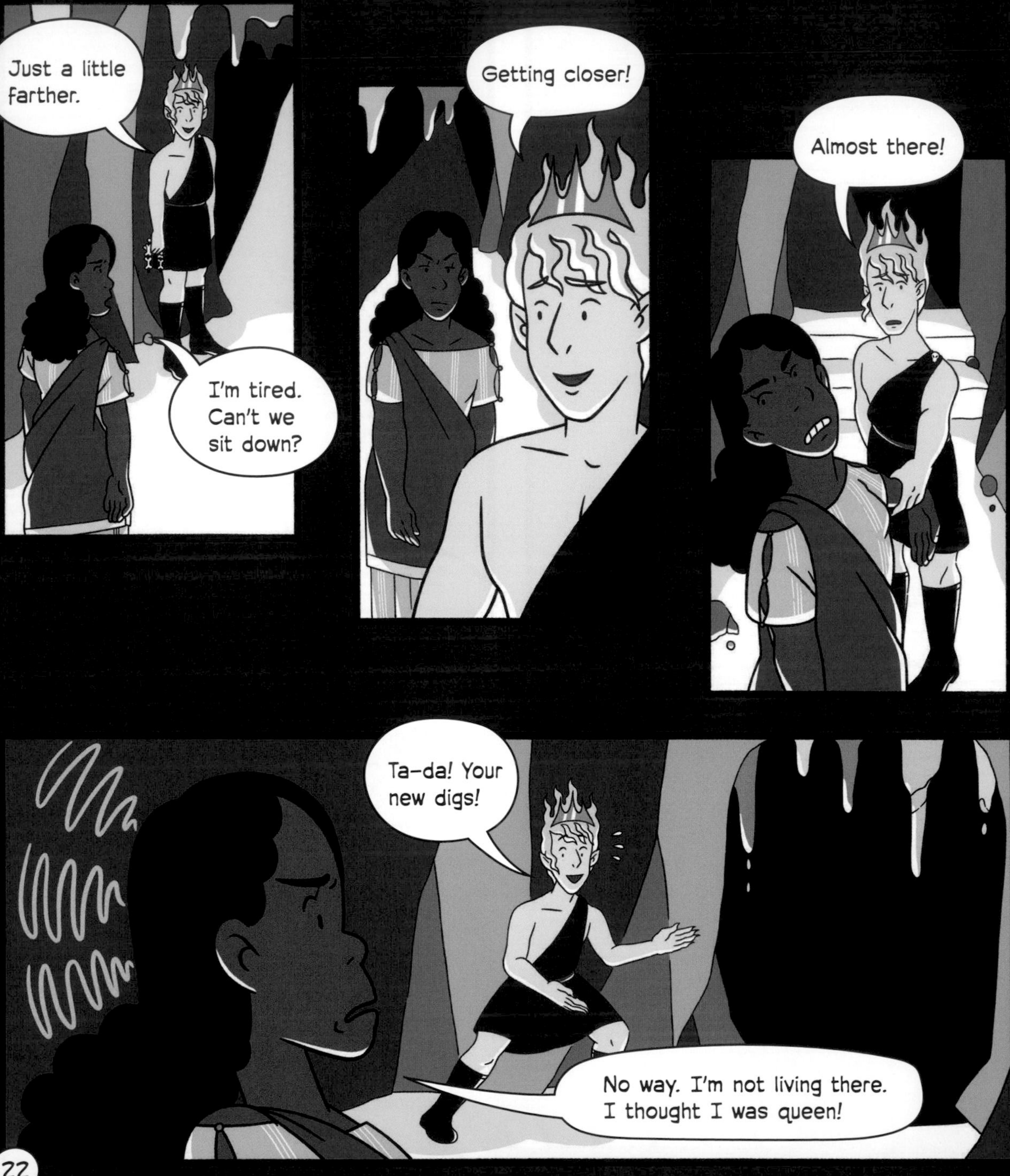
Just a little farther.
I'm tired. Can't we sit down?
Getting closer!
Almost there!
Ta-da! Your new digs!
No way. I'm not living there. I thought I was queen!

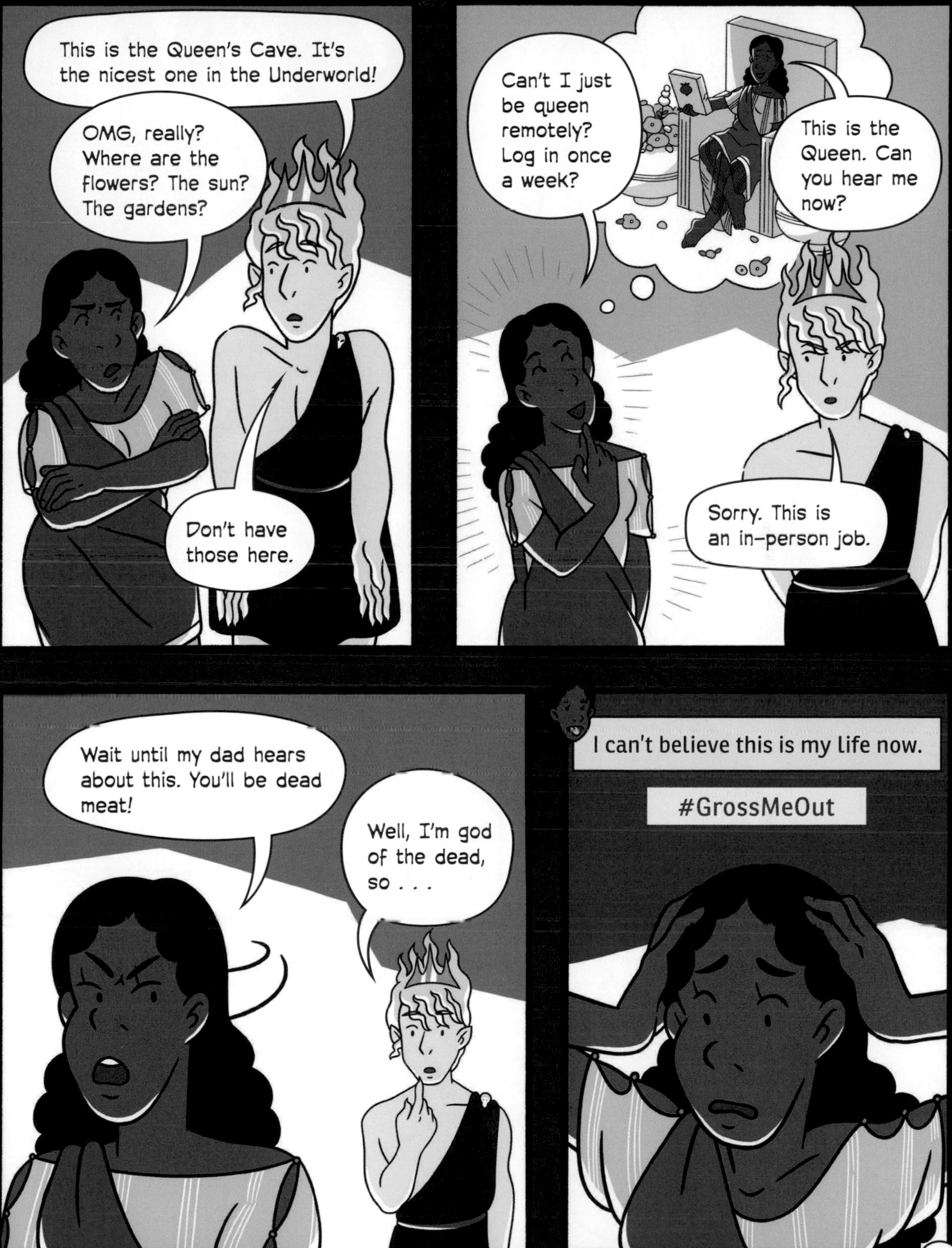
This is the Queen's Cave. It's the nicest one in the Underworld!
OMG, really? Where are the flowers? The sun? The gardens?
Don't have those here.
Can't I just be queen remotely? Log in once a week?
This is the Queen. Can you hear me now?
Sorry. This is an in-person job.
Wait until my dad hears about this. You'll be dead meat!
Well, I'm god of the dead, so . . .
I can't believe this is my life now.
#GrossMeOut

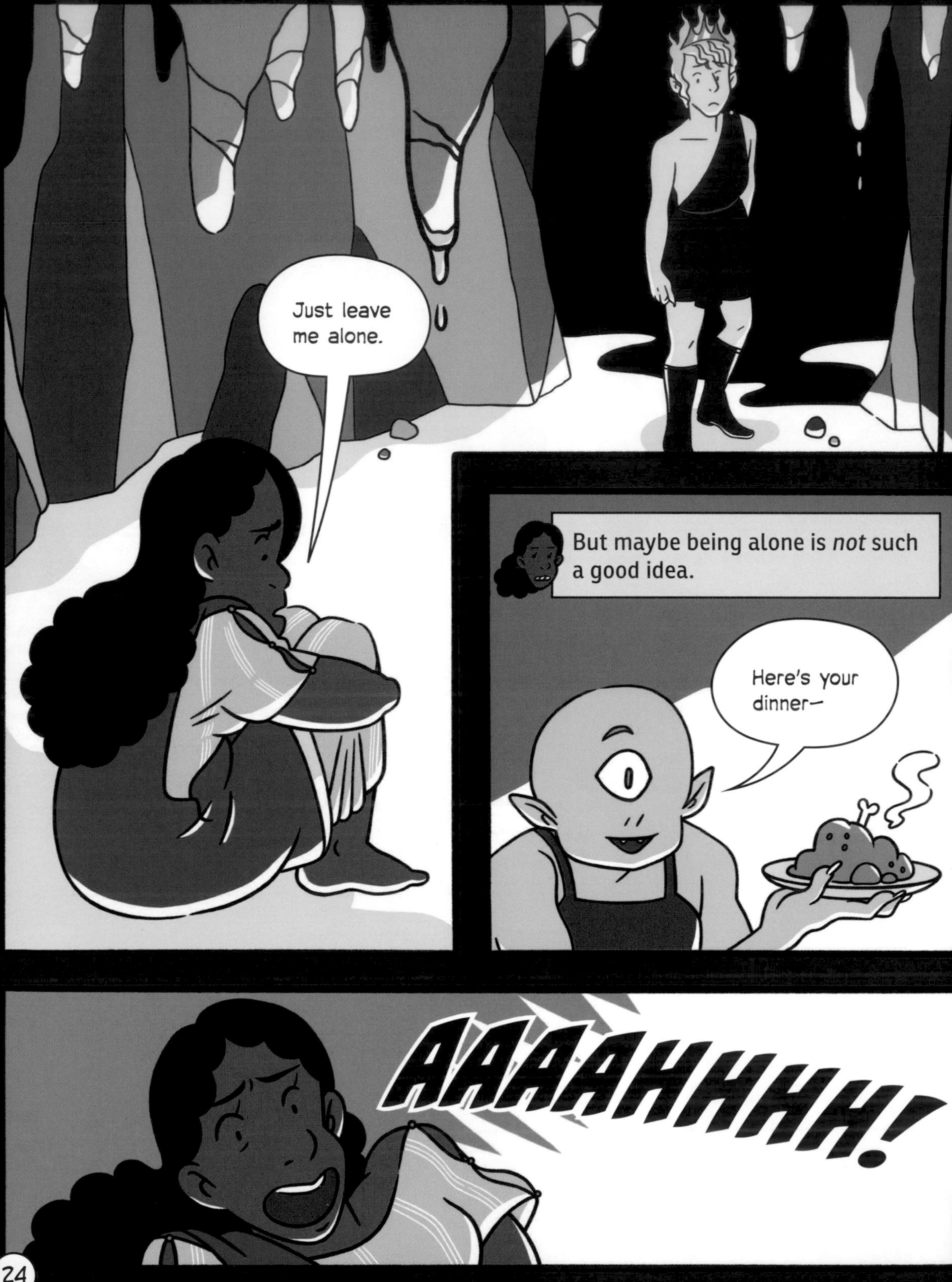
Just leave me alone.
But maybe being alone is *not* such a good idea.
Here's your dinner—
AAAAHHHH!

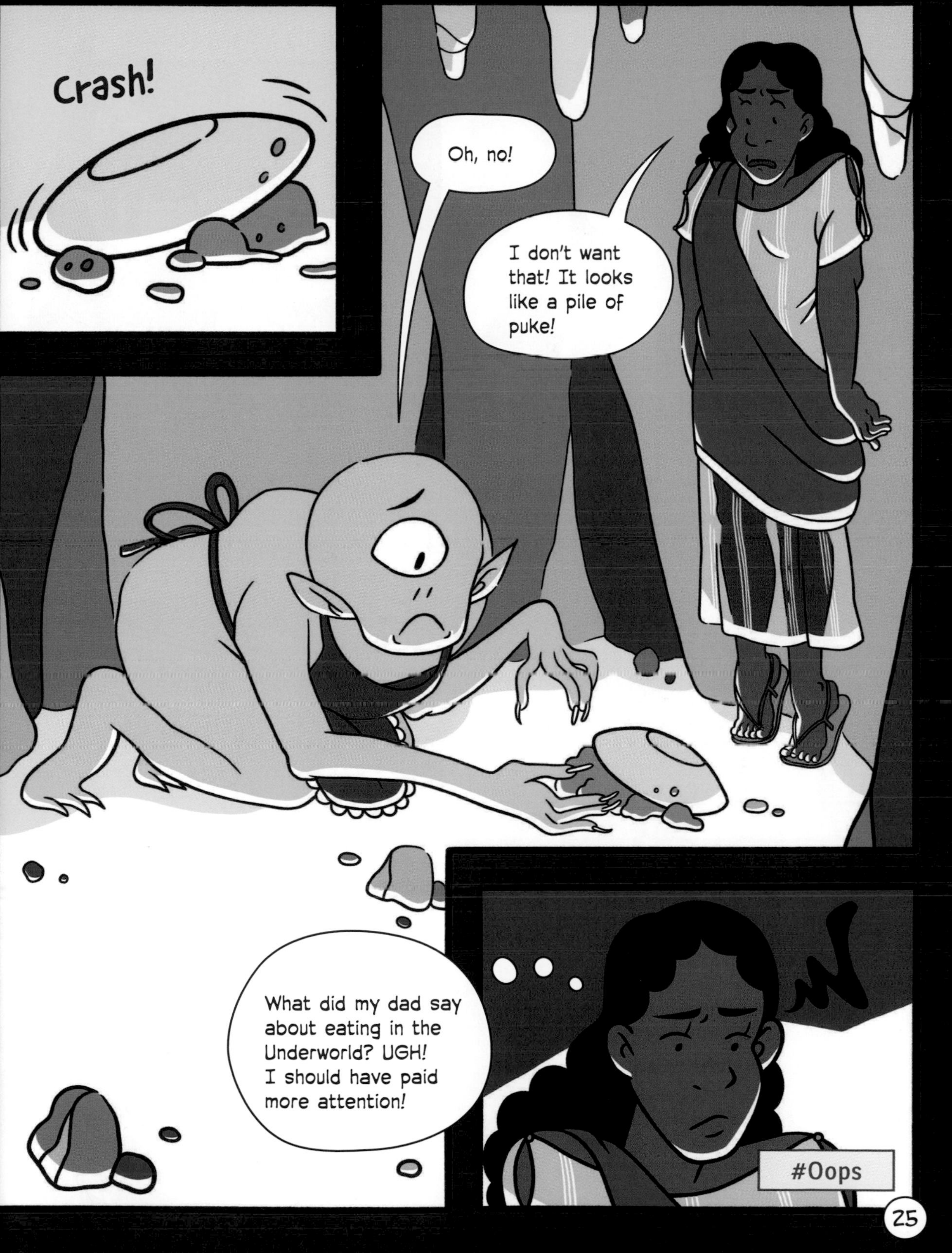
Crash!
Oh, no!
I don't want that! It looks like a pile of puke!
What did my dad say about eating in the Underworld? UGH! I should have paid more attention!
#Oops

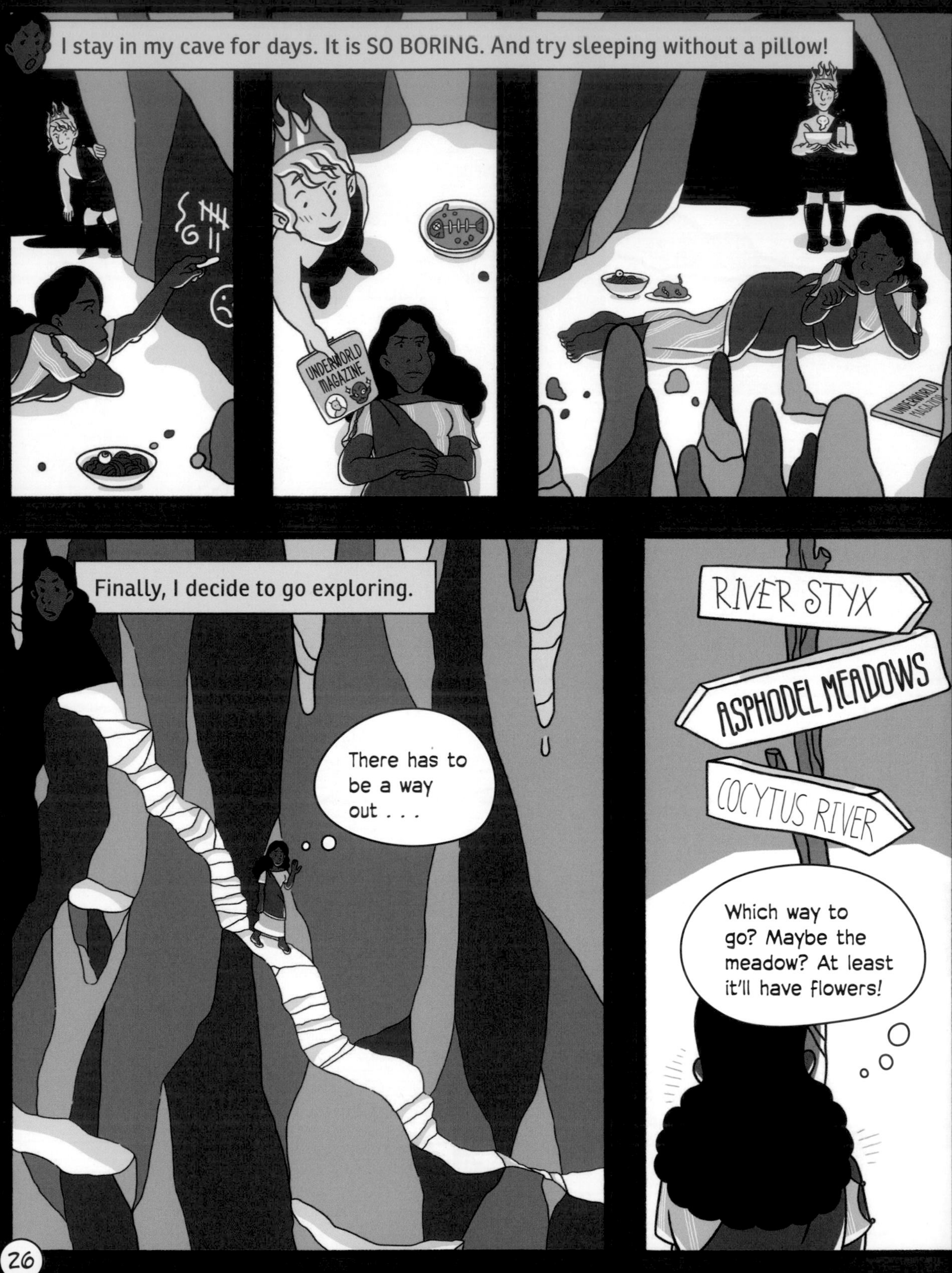
I stay in my cave for days. It is SO BORING. And try sleeping without a pillow!
UNDERWORLD MAGAZINE
UNDERWORLD MAGAZINE
Finally, I decide to go exploring.
There has to be a way out . . .
RIVER STYX
ASPHODEL MEADOWS
COCYTUS RIVER
Which way to go? Maybe the meadow? At least it'll have flowers!

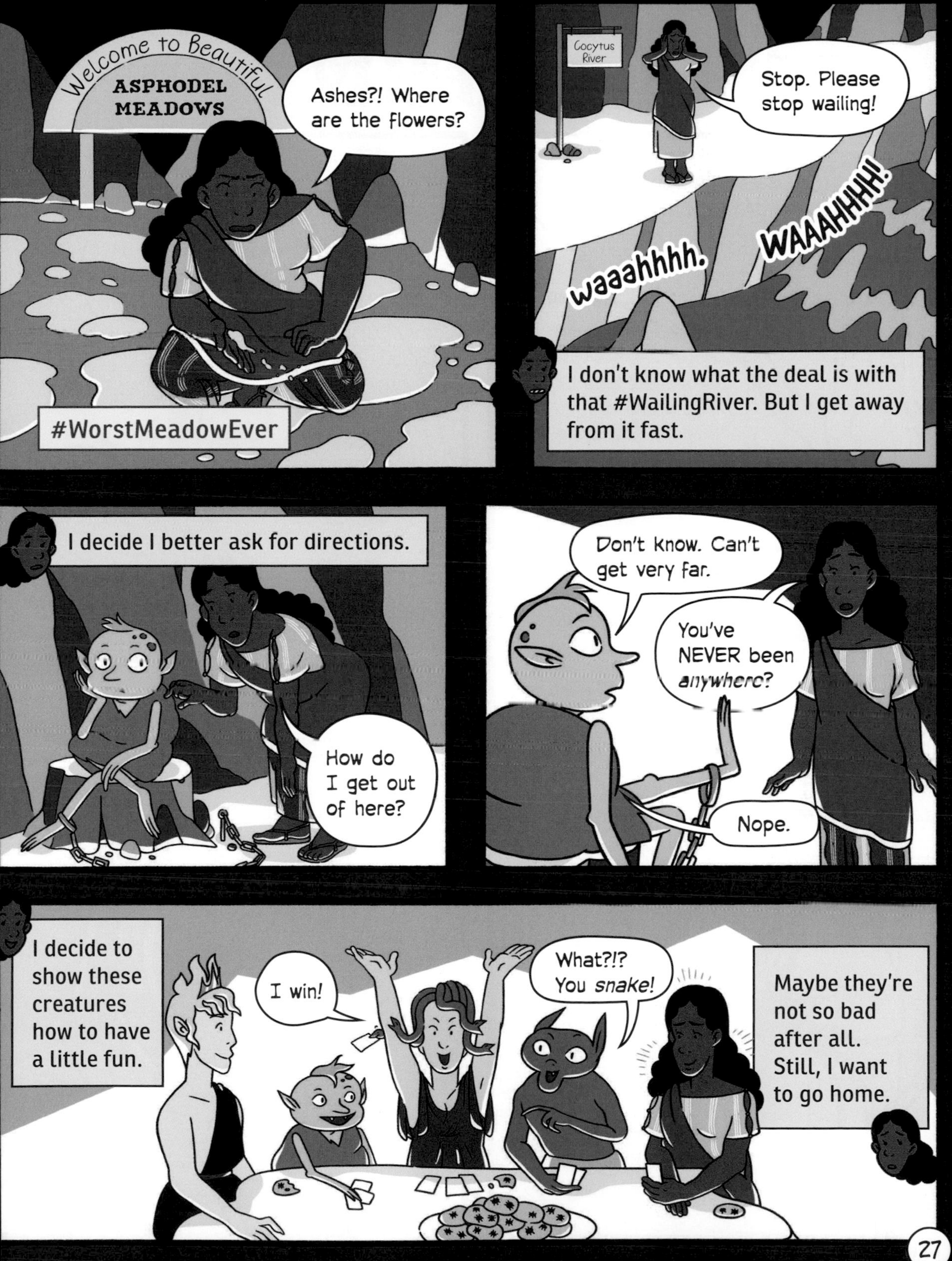
Welcome to Beautiful
ASPHODEL MEADOWS
Ashes?! Where are the flowers?
#WorstMeadowEver
Cocytus River
Stop. Please stop wailing!
waaahhhh.
WAAAHHHH!
I don't know what the deal is with that #WailingRiver. But I get away from it fast.
I decide I better ask for directions.
How do I get out of here?
Don't know. Can't get very far.
You've NEVER been *anywhere*?
Nope.
I decide to show these creatures how to have a little fun.
I win!
What?!? You *snake*!
Maybe they're not so bad after all. Still, I want to go home.

CHAPTER 4

MOM IS REALLY MAD

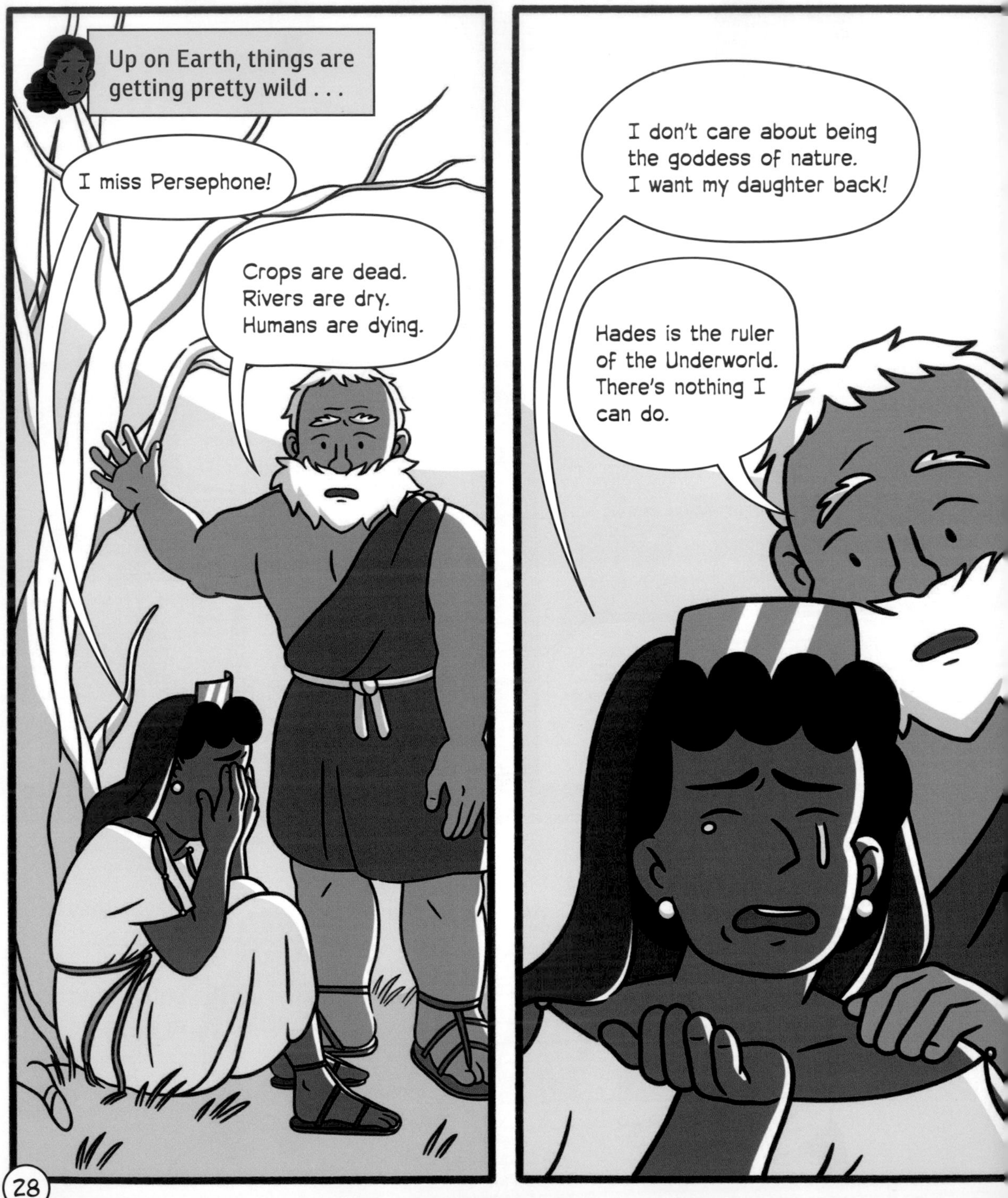
Up on Earth, things are getting pretty wild . . .
I miss Persephone!
Crops are dead. Rivers are dry. Humans are dying.
I don't care about being the goddess of nature. I want my daughter back!
Hades is the ruler of the Underworld. There's nothing I can do.

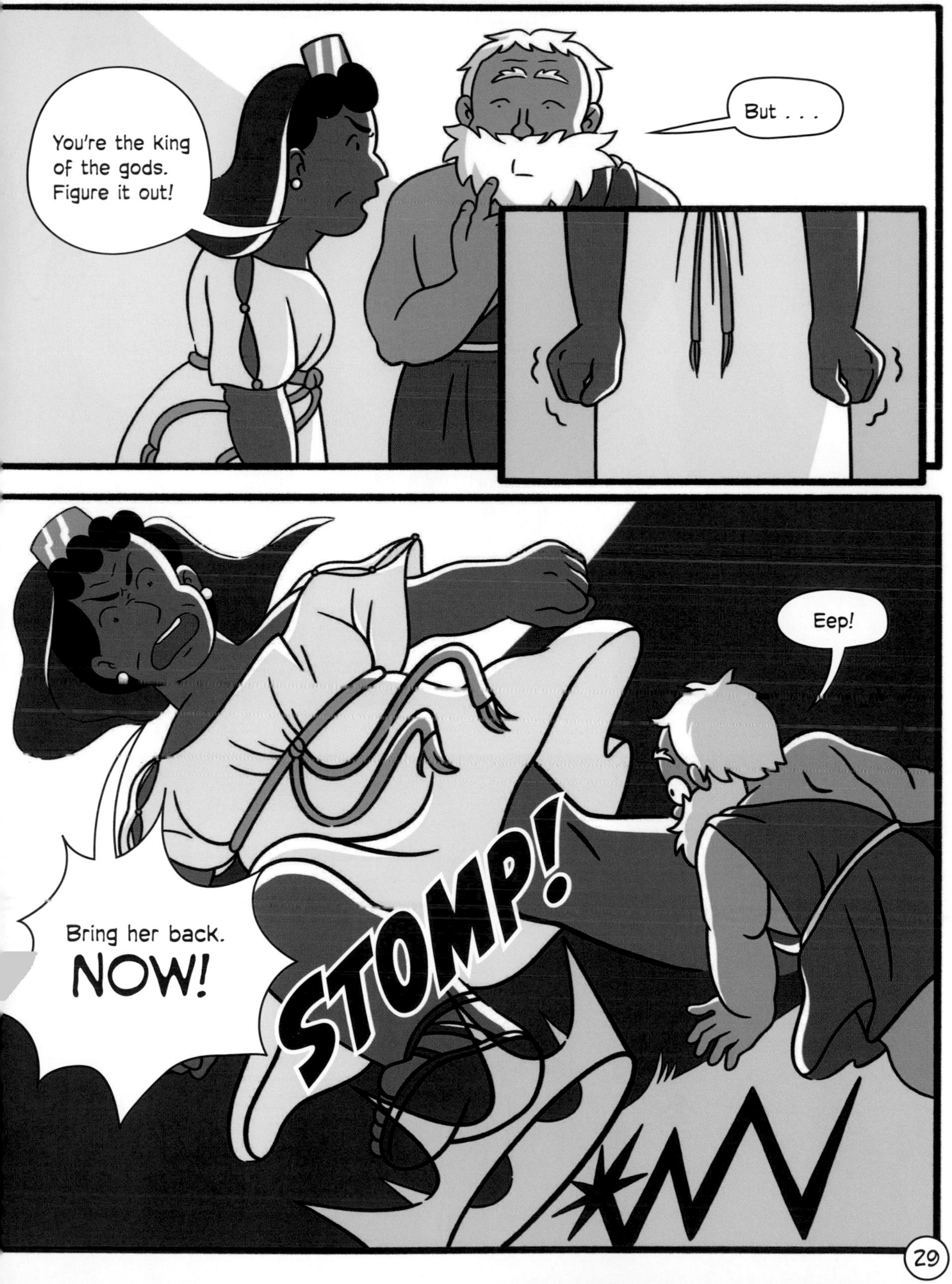
You're the king of the gods. Figure it out!
But . . .
Eep!
Bring her back. NOW!
STOMP!

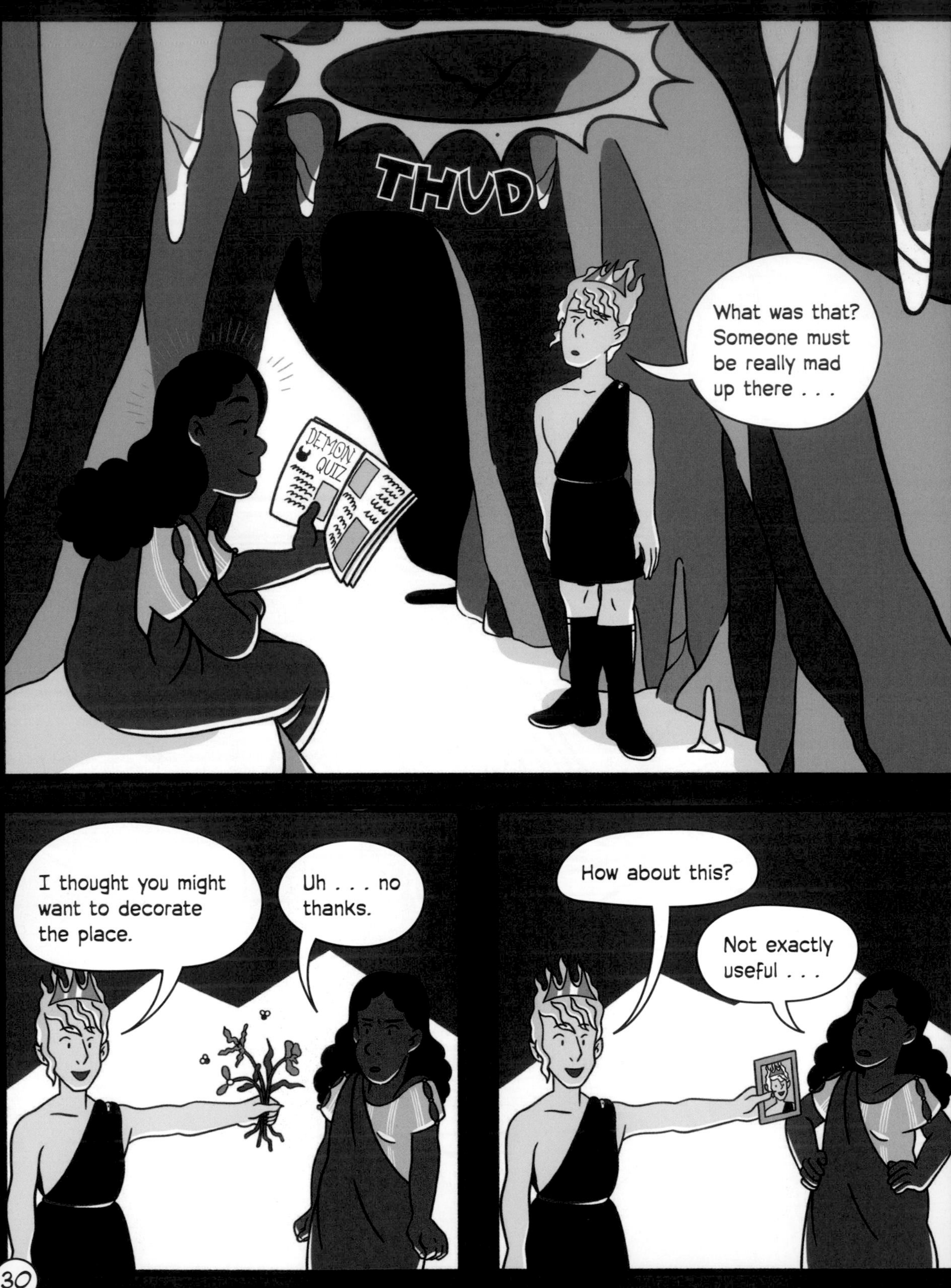
THUD
DEMON QUIZ
What was that? Someone must be really mad up there . . .
I thought you might want to decorate the place.
Uh . . . no thanks.
How about this?
Not exactly useful . . .

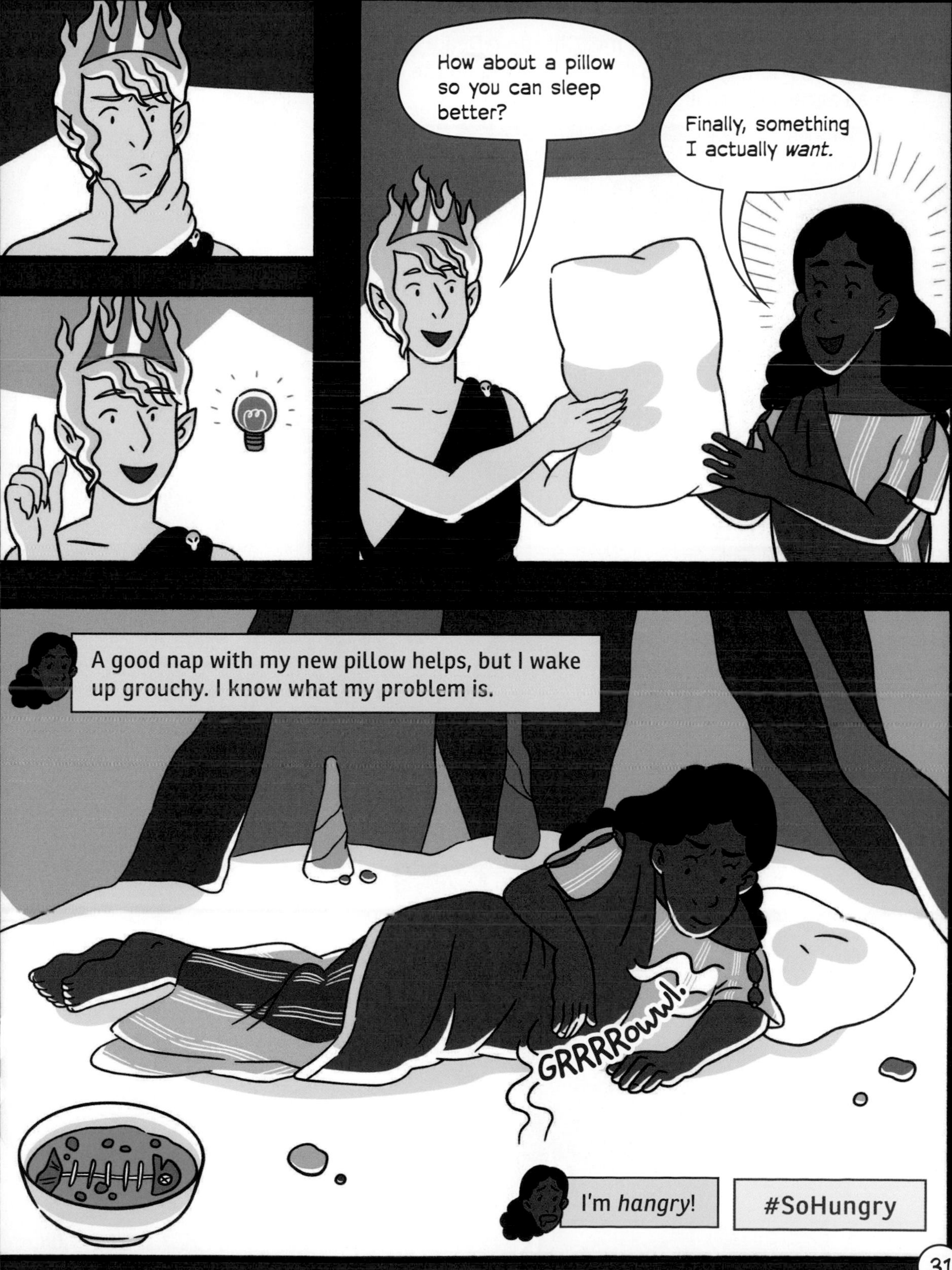
How about a pillow so you can sleep better?
Finally, something I actually *want.*
A good nap with my new pillow helps, but I wake up grouchy. I know what my problem is.
GRRRRowwl!
I'm *hangry*!
#SoHungry

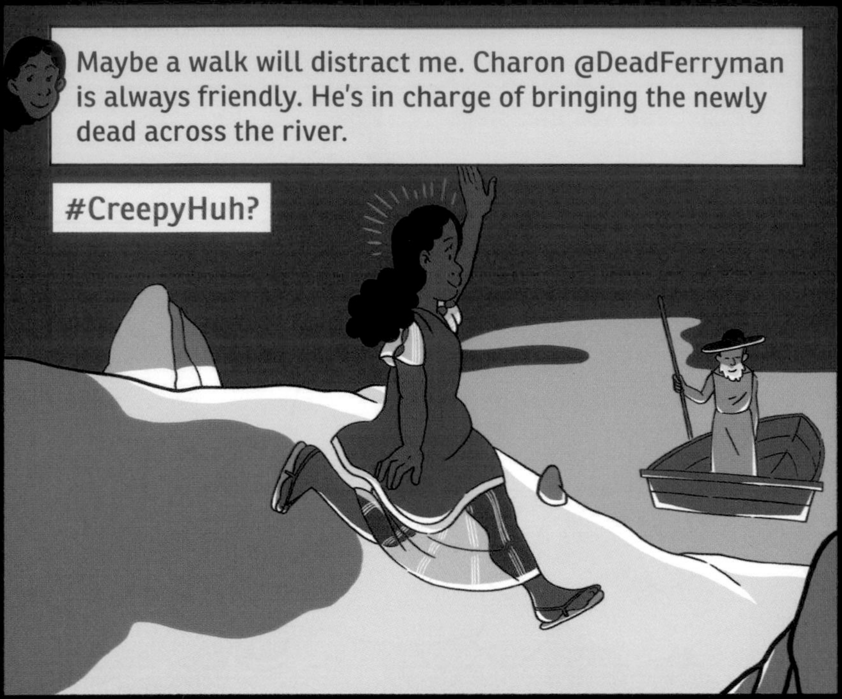
Maybe a walk will distract me. Charon @DeadFerryman is always friendly. He's in charge of bringing the newly dead across the river.
#CreepyHuh?

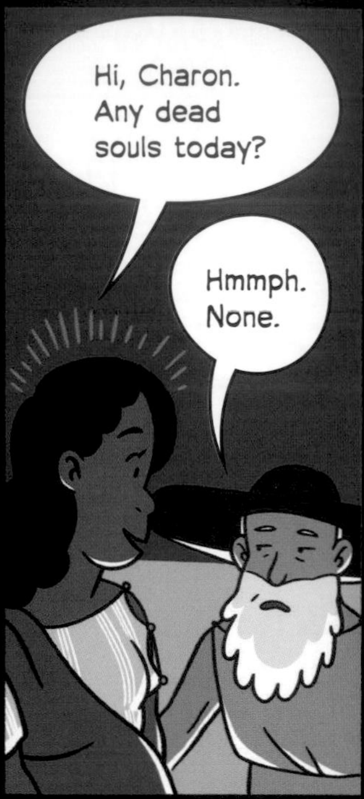
Hi, Charon. Any dead souls today?
Hmmph. None.

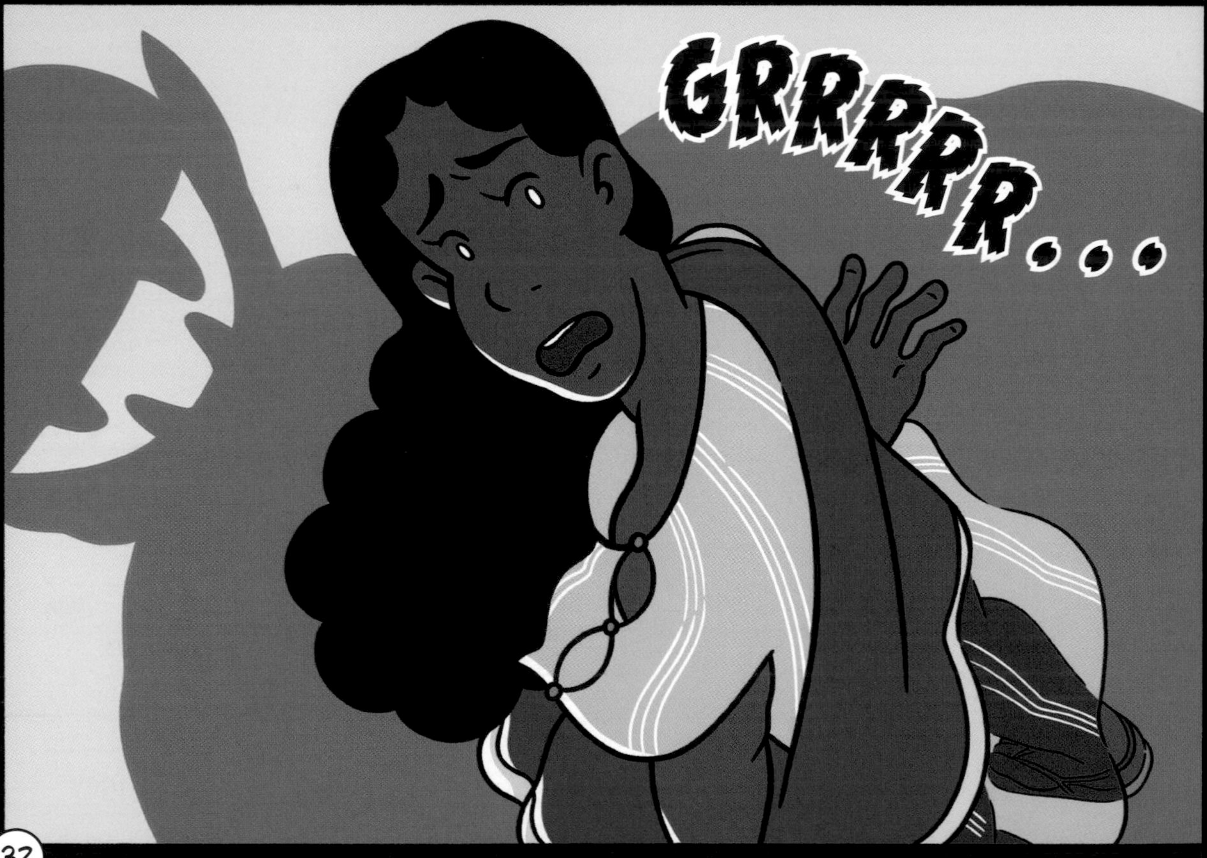
GRRRRR...

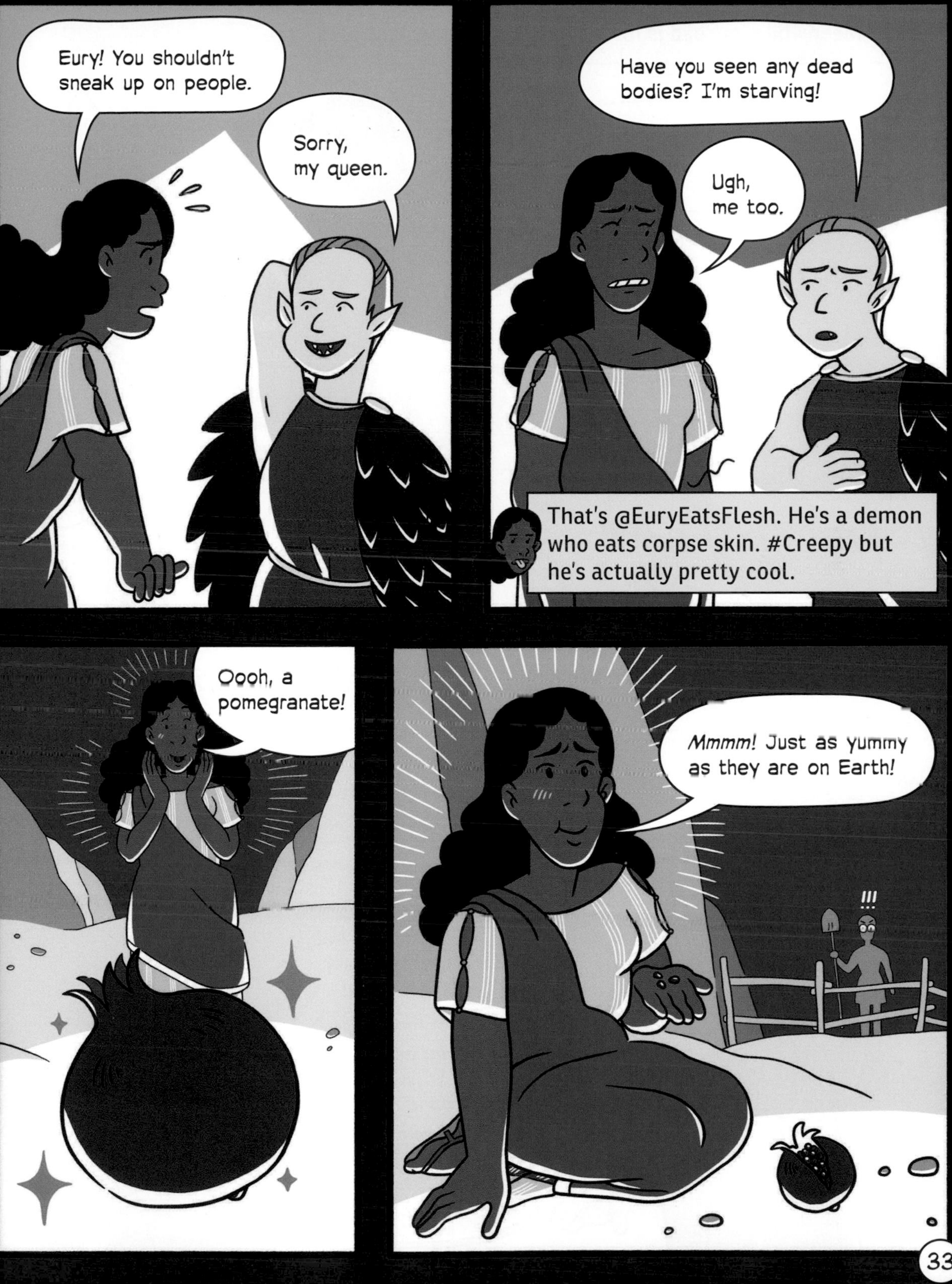
Eury! You shouldn't sneak up on people.
Sorry, my queen.
Have you seen any dead bodies? I'm starving!
Ugh, me too.
That's @EuryEatsFlesh. He's a demon who eats corpse skin. #Creepy but he's actually pretty cool.
Oooh, a pomegranate!
Mmmm! Just as yummy as they are on Earth!
!!!

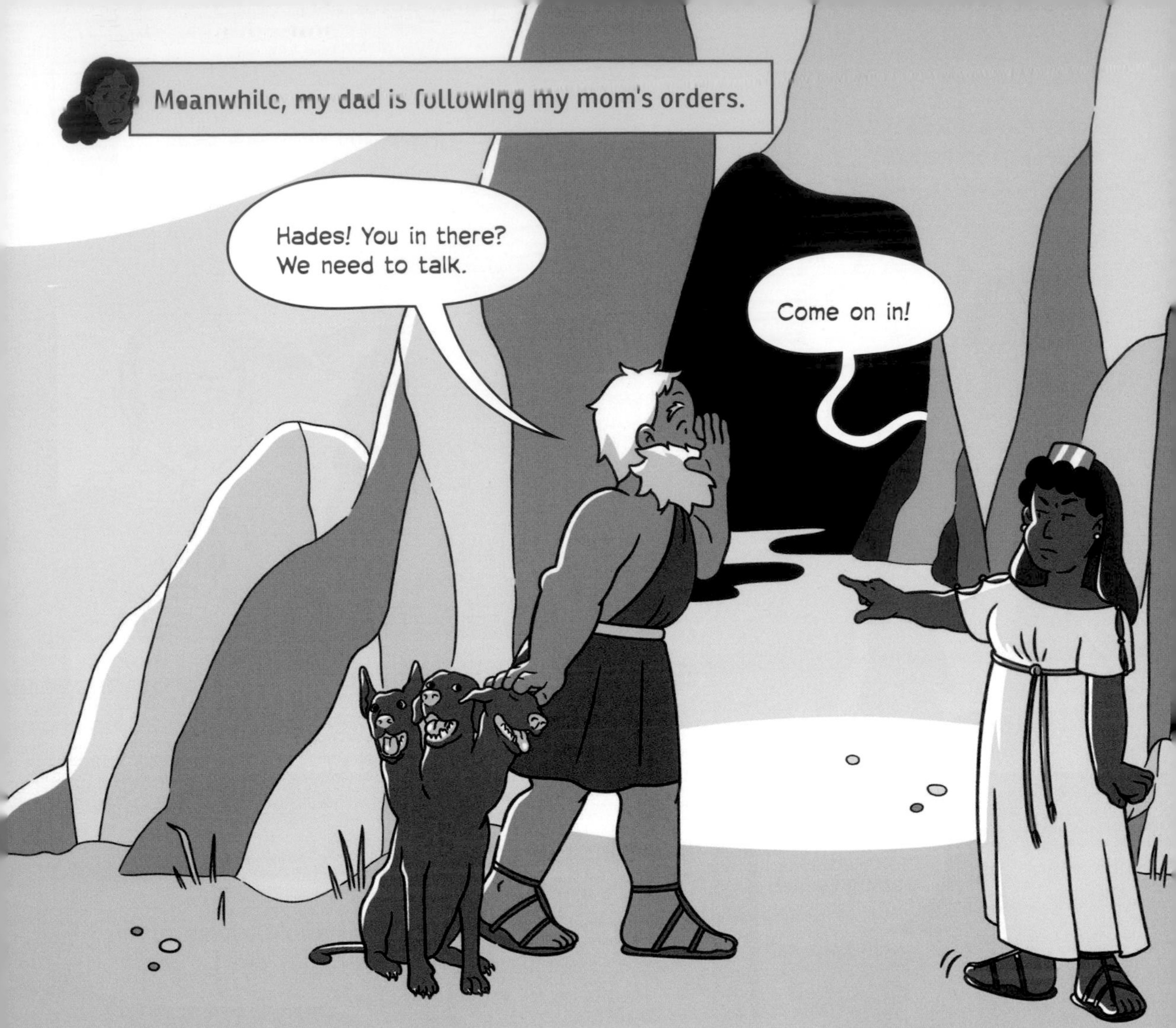
Meanwhile, my dad is following my mom's orders.
Hades! You in there? We need to talk.
Come on in!

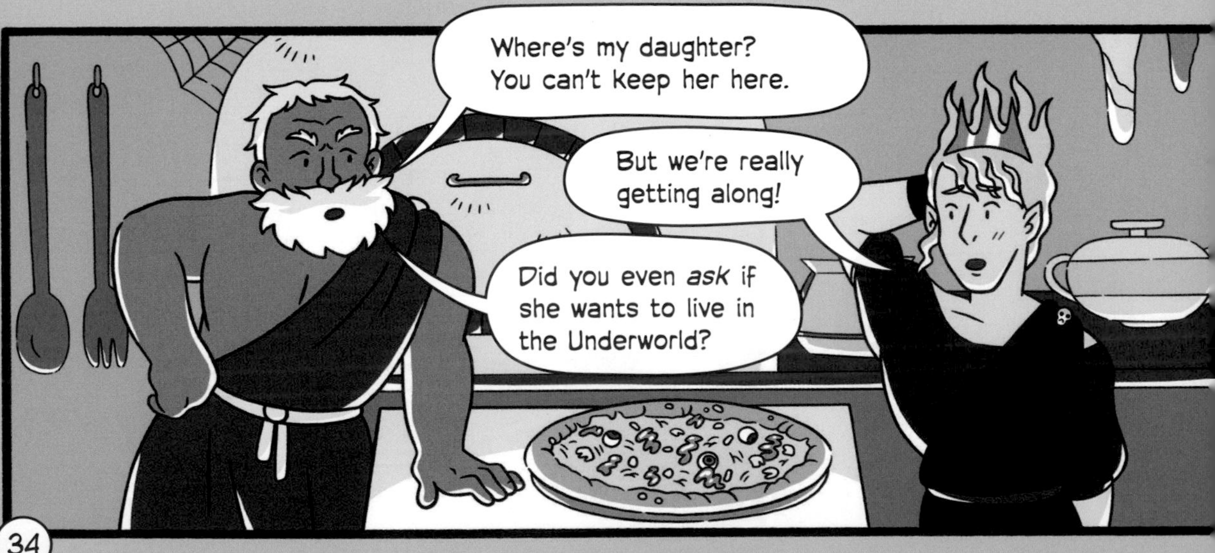
Where's my daughter? You can't keep her here.
But we're really getting along!
Did you even *ask* if she wants to live in the Underworld?

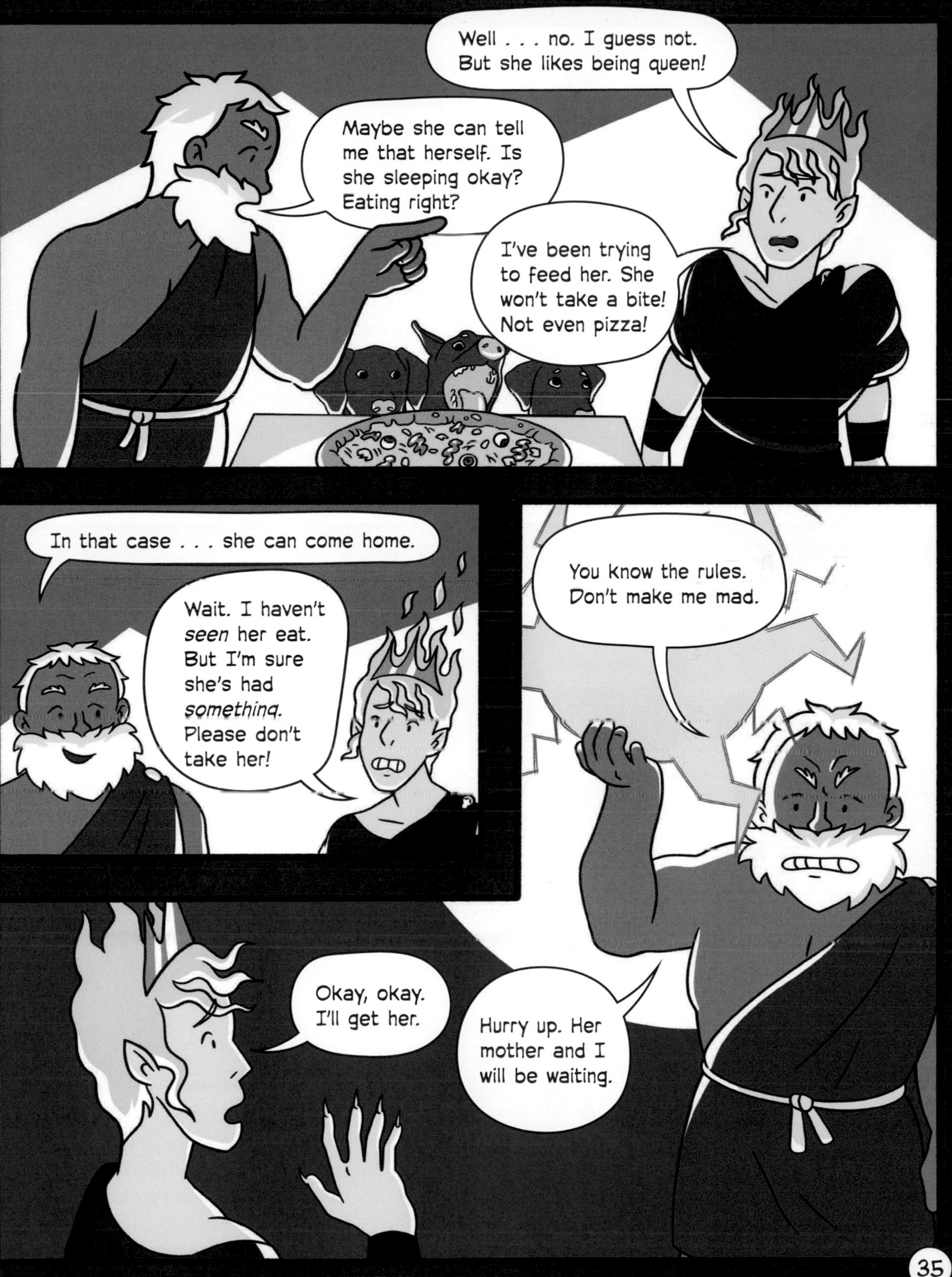
Maybe she can tell me that herself. Is she sleeping okay? Eating right?
Well . . . no. I guess not. But she likes being queen!
I've been trying to feed her. She won't take a bite! Not even pizza!
In that case . . . she can come home.
Wait. I haven't *seen* her eat. But I'm sure she's had *something*. Please don't take her!
You know the rules. Don't make me mad.
Okay, okay. I'll get her.
Hurry up. Her mother and I will be waiting.

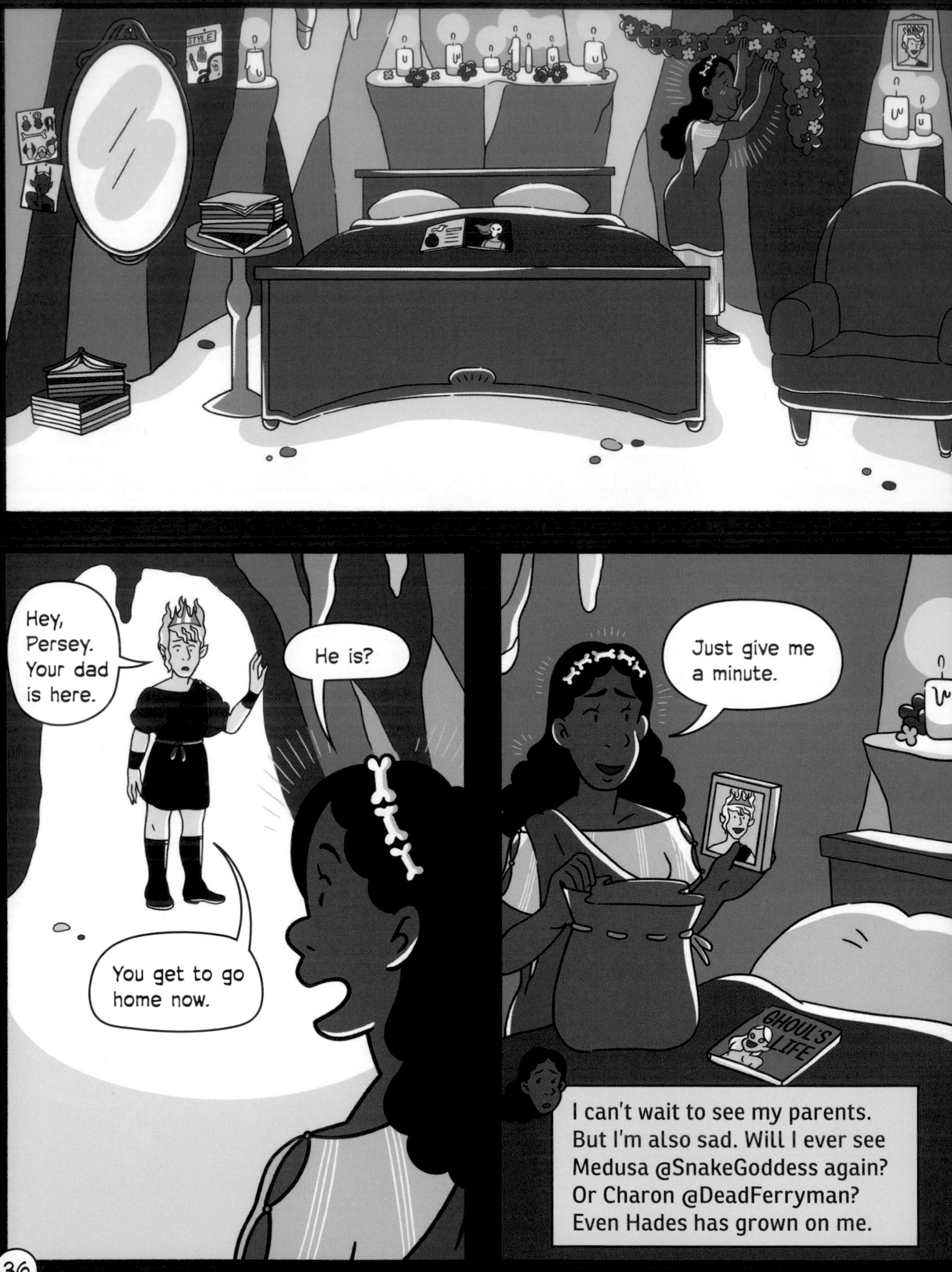
STYLE
Hey, Persey. Your dad is here.
He is?
You get to go home now.
Just give me a minute.
GHOUL'S LIFE
I can't wait to see my parents. But I'm also sad. Will I ever see Medusa @SnakeGoddess again? Or Charon @DeadFerryman? Even Hades has grown on me.

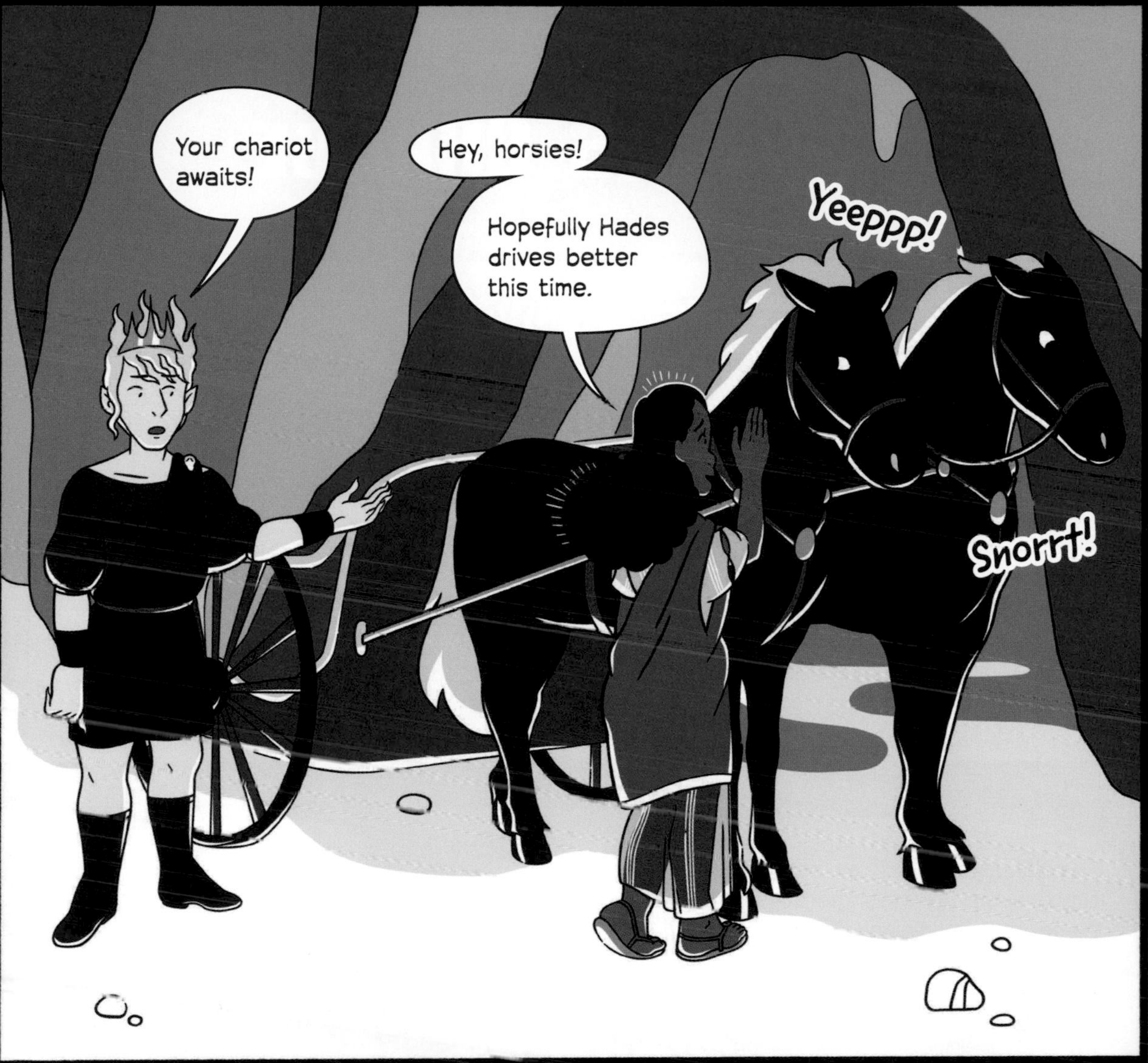
Your chariot awaits!
Hey, horsies!
Hopefully Hades drives better this time.
Yeeppp!
Snorrt!

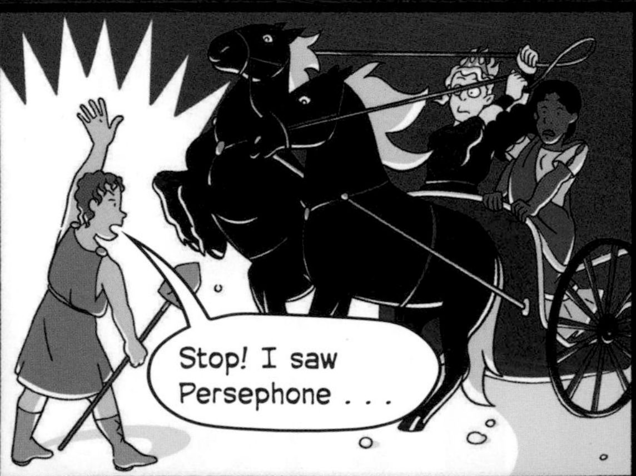
Stop! I saw Persephone . . .

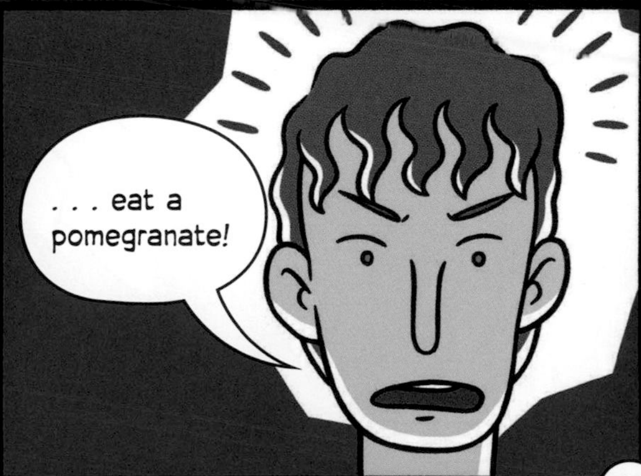
. . . eat a pomegranate!

CHAPTER 5

SEASONS CHANGE

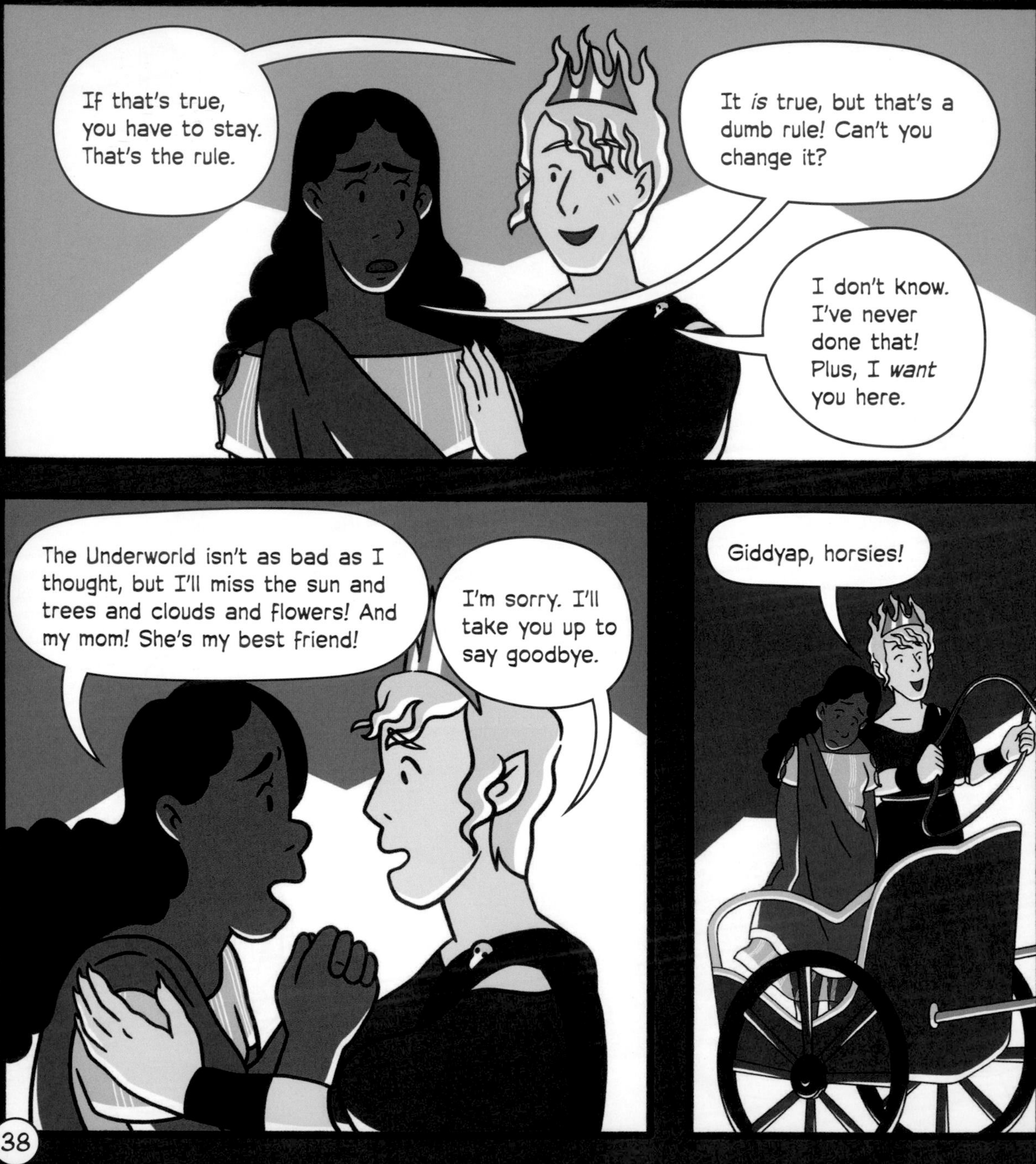
If that's true, you have to stay. That's the rule.
It *is* true, but that's a dumb rule! Can't you change it?
I don't know. I've never done that! Plus, I *want* you here.
The Underworld isn't as bad as I thought, but I'll miss the sun and trees and clouds and flowers! And my mom! She's my best friend!
I'm sorry. I'll take you up to say goodbye.
Giddyap, horsies!

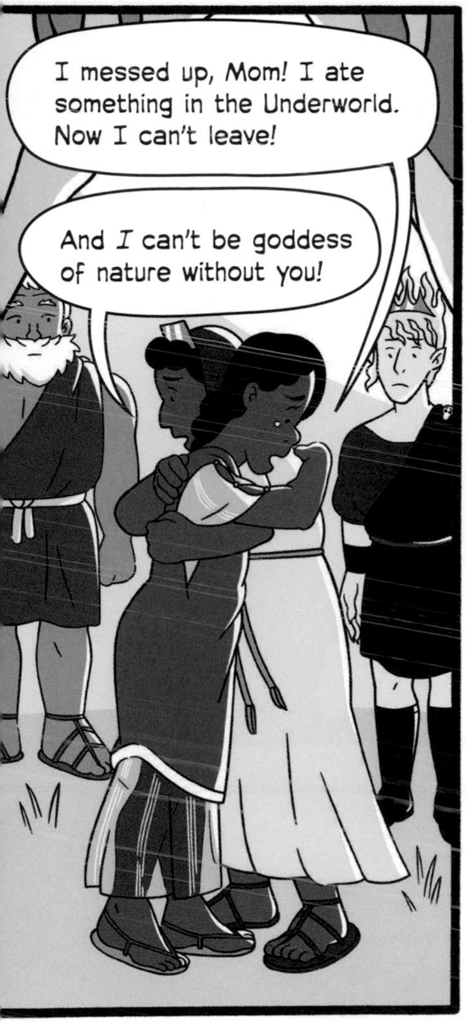
I messed up, Mom! I ate something in the Underworld. Now I can't leave!
And *I* can't be goddess of nature without you!

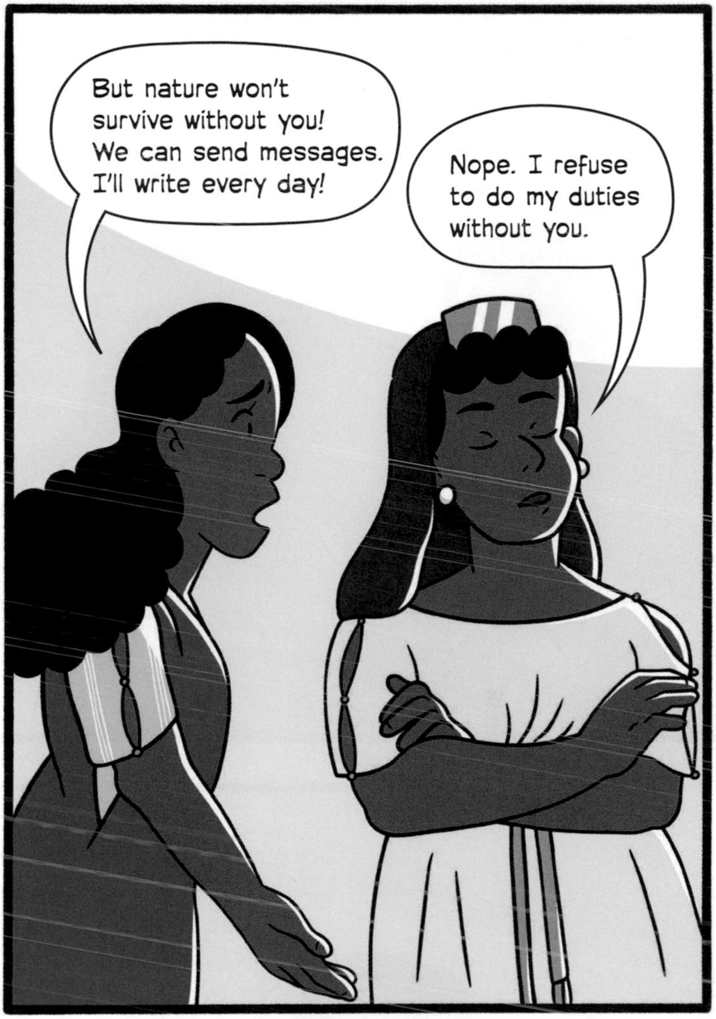
But nature won't survive without you! We can send messages. I'll write every day!
Nope. I refuse to do my duties without you.

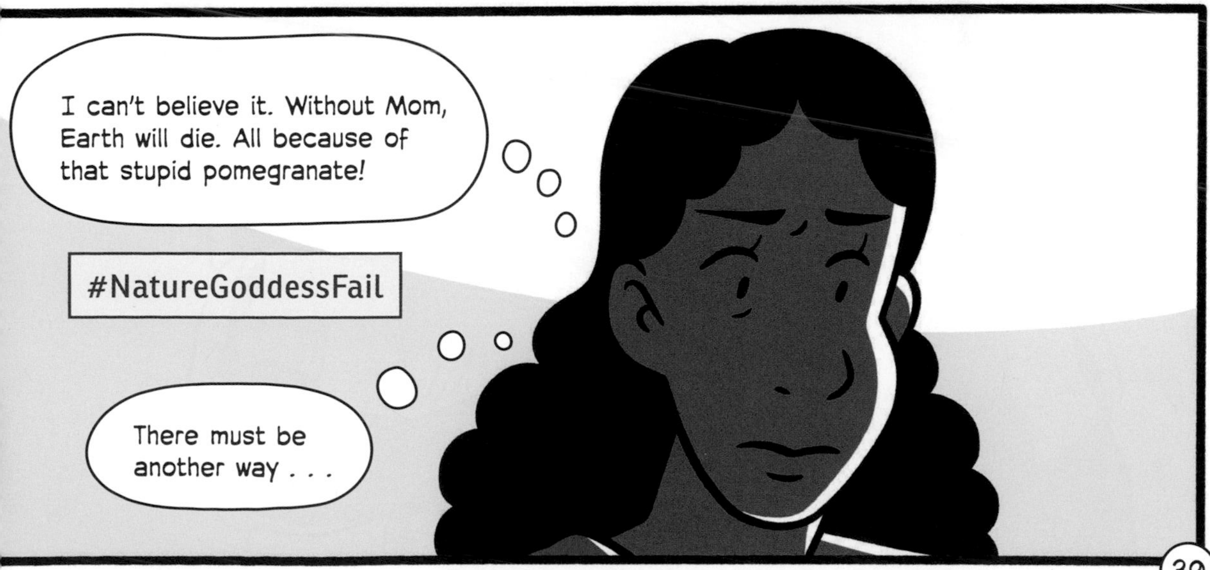
I can't believe it. Without Mom, Earth will die. All because of that stupid pomegranate!
#NatureGoddessFail
There must be another way . . .

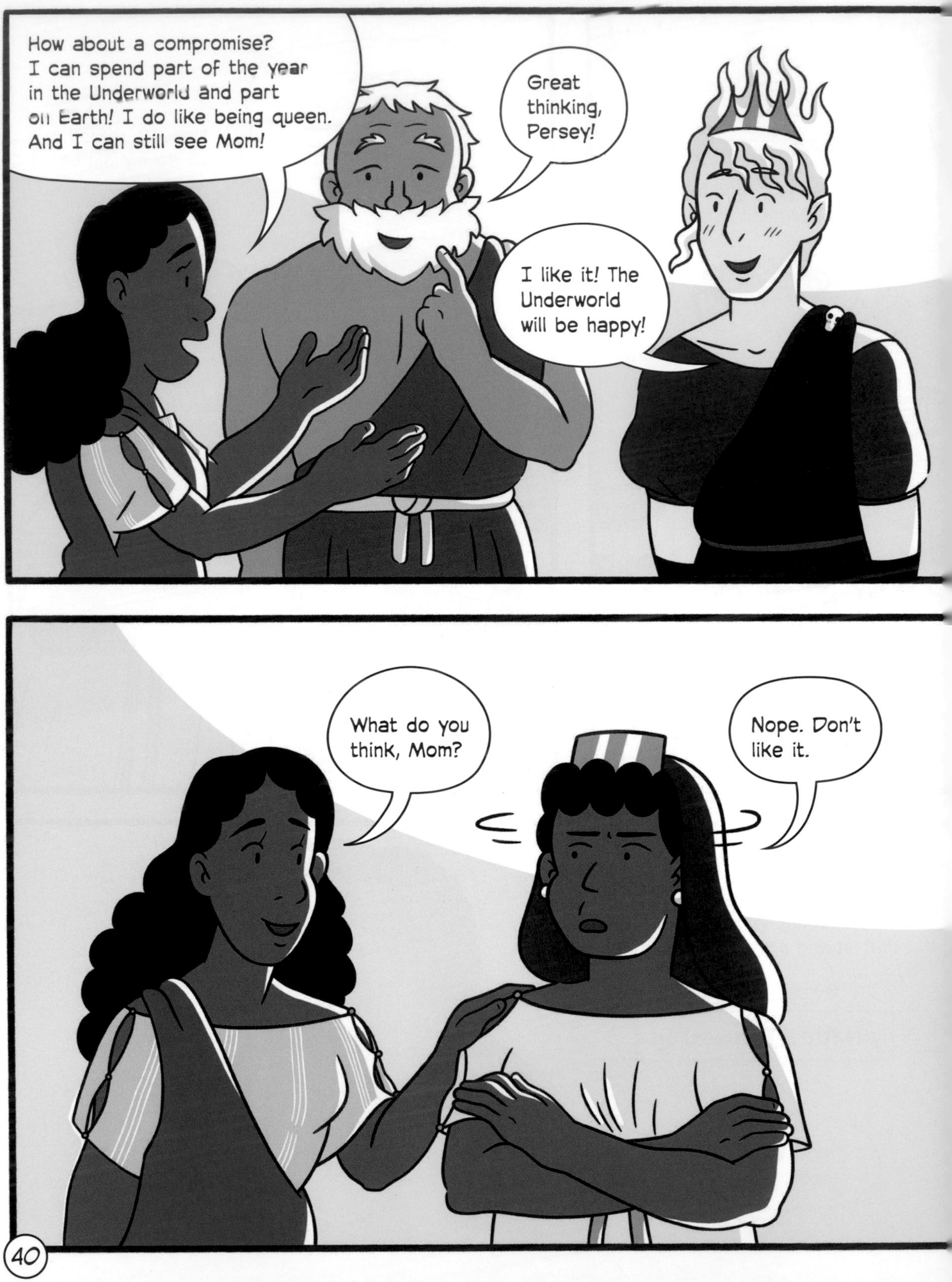
How about a compromise? I can spend part of the year in the Underworld and part on Earth! I do like being queen. And I can still see Mom!
Great thinking, Persey!
I like it! The Underworld will be happy!
What do you think, Mom?
Nope. Don't like it.

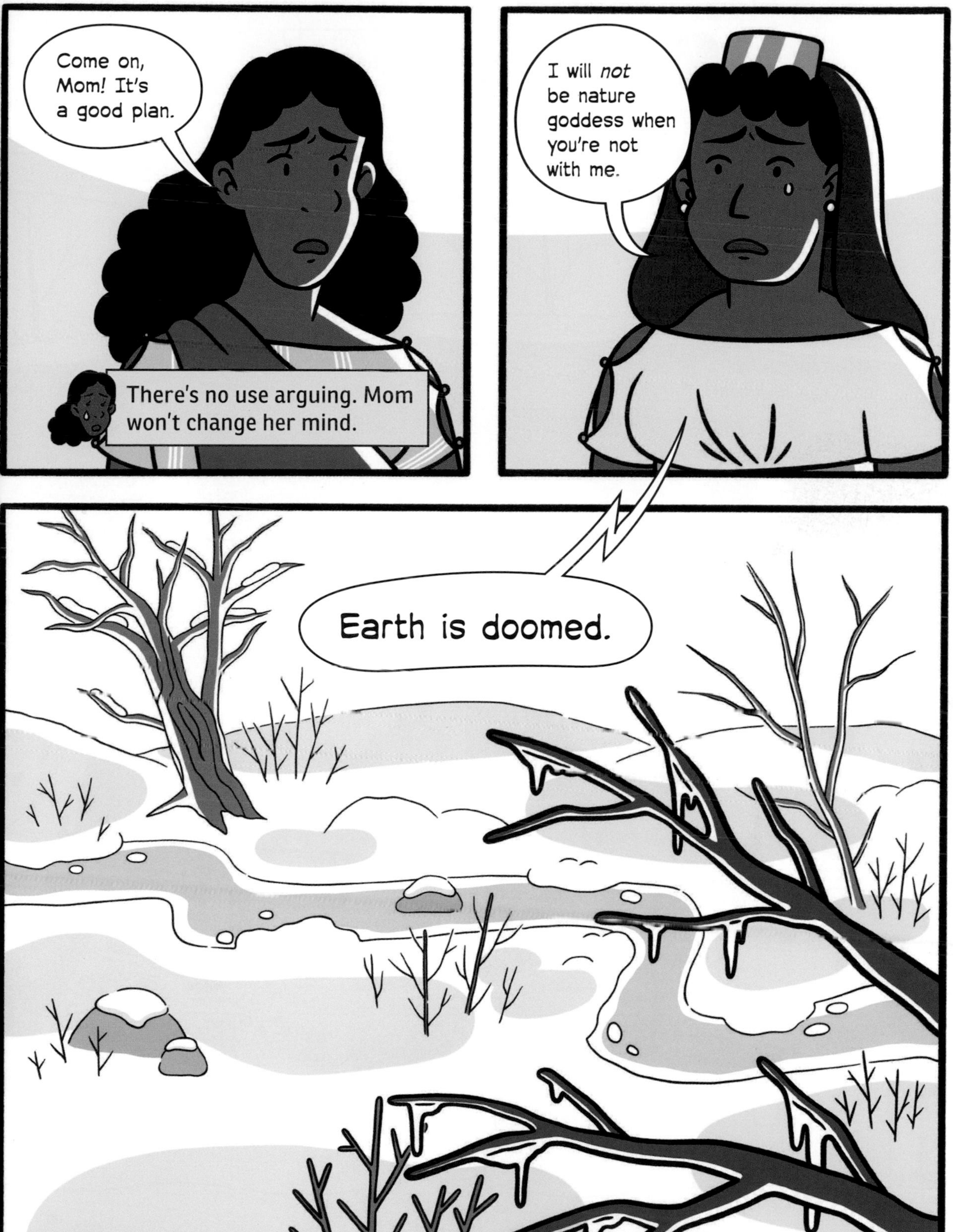
Come on, Mom! It's a good plan.
There's no use arguing. Mom won't change her mind.
I will *not* be nature goddess when you're not with me.
Earth is doomed.

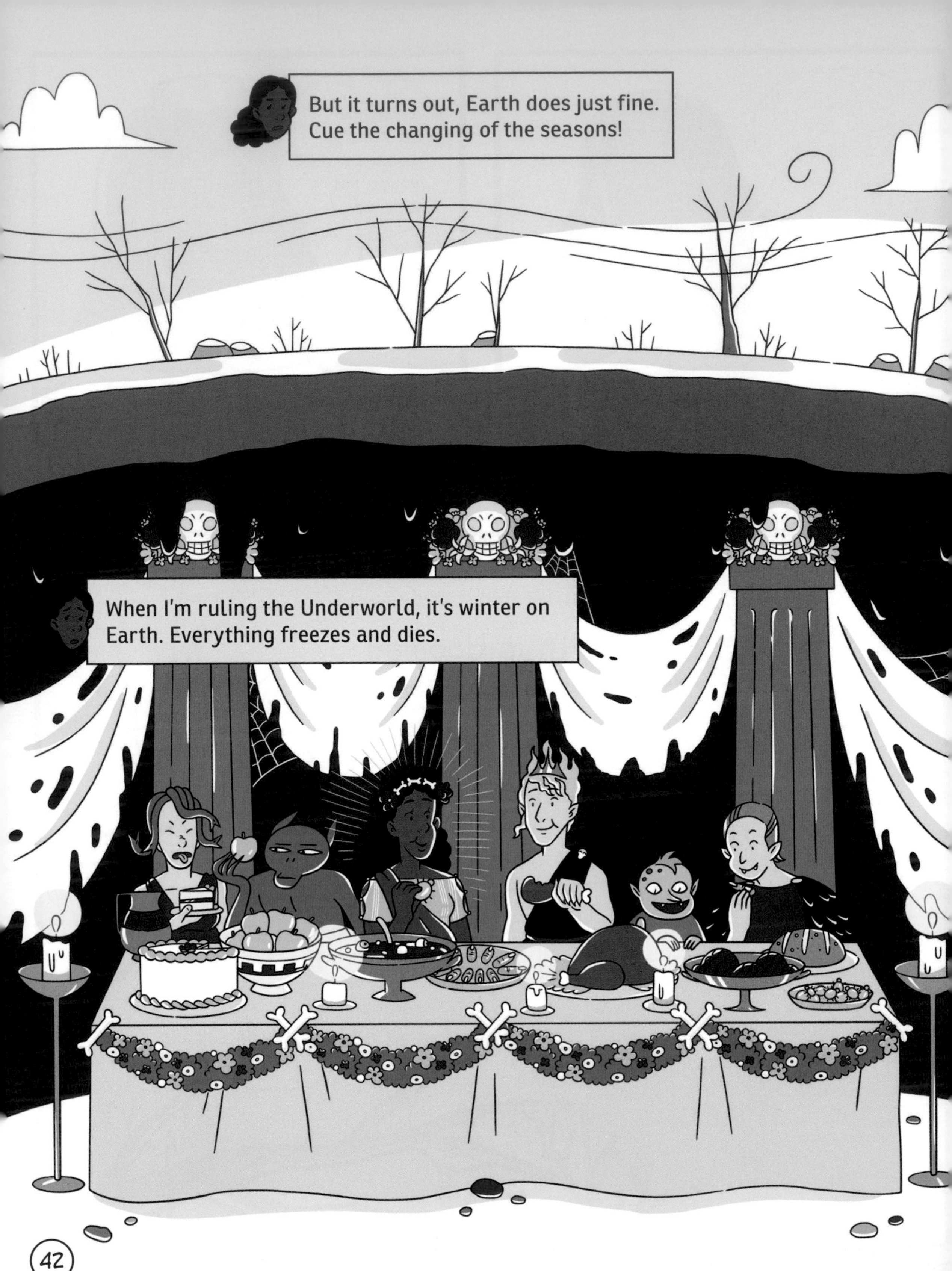

But it turns out, Earth does just fine. Cue the changing of the seasons!
When I'm ruling the Underworld, it's winter on Earth. Everything freezes and dies.

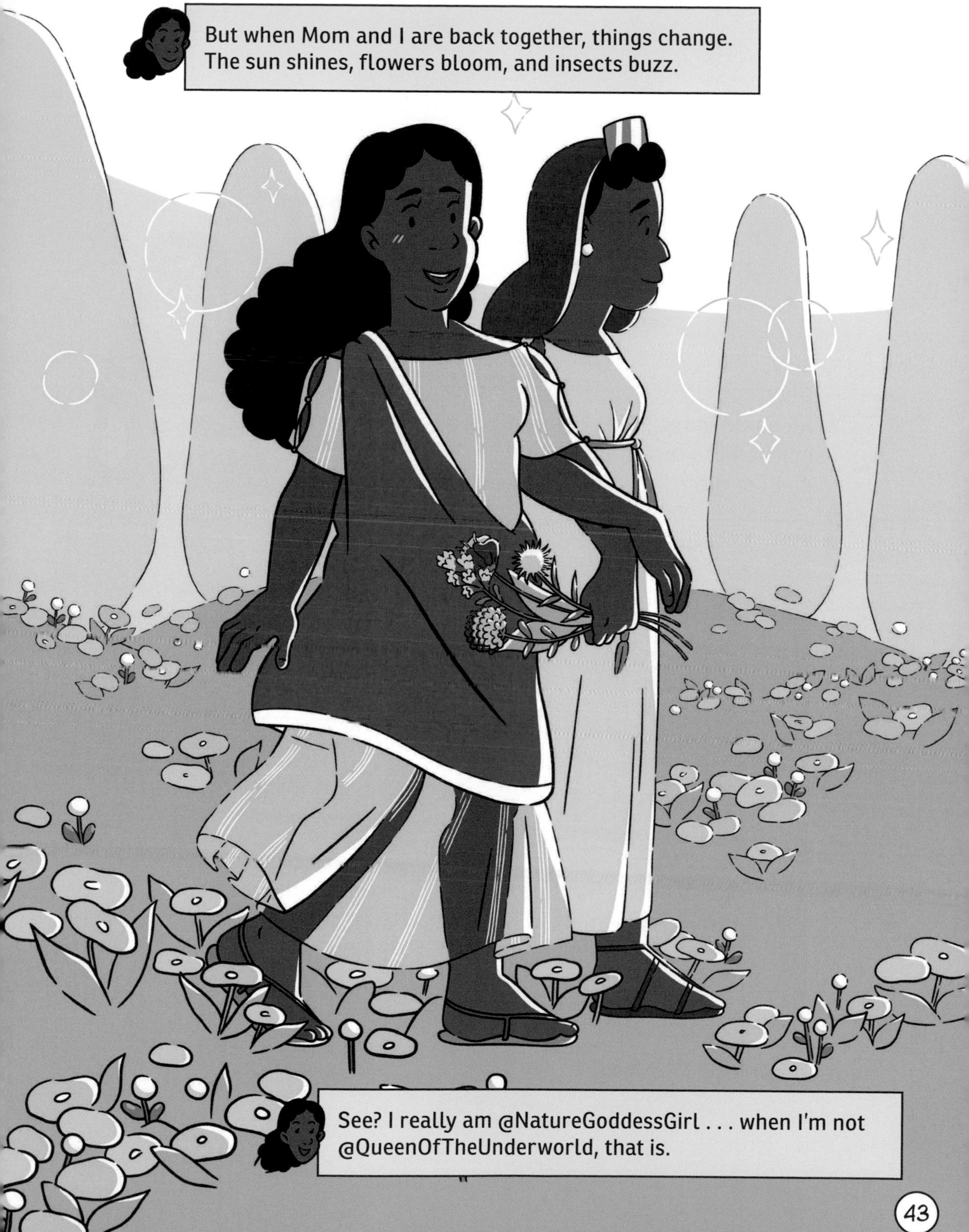
But when Mom and I are back together, things change. The sun shines, flowers bloom, and insects buzz.
See? I really am @NatureGoddessGirl . . . when I'm not @QueenOfTheUnderworld, that is.

More About Persephone

The name Persephone comes from an ancient word meaning "ear of corn" or "sheaf of grain."

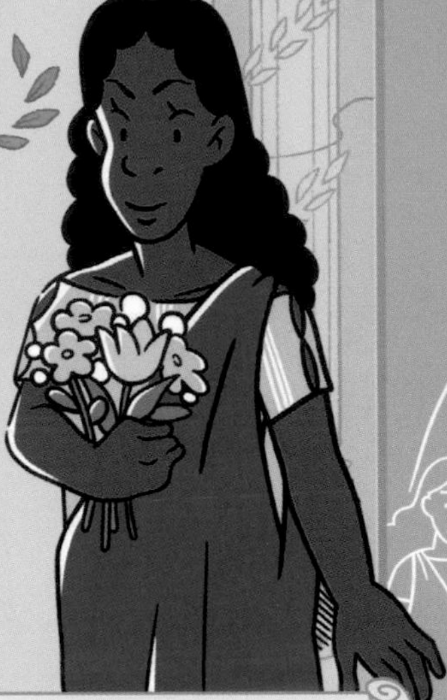

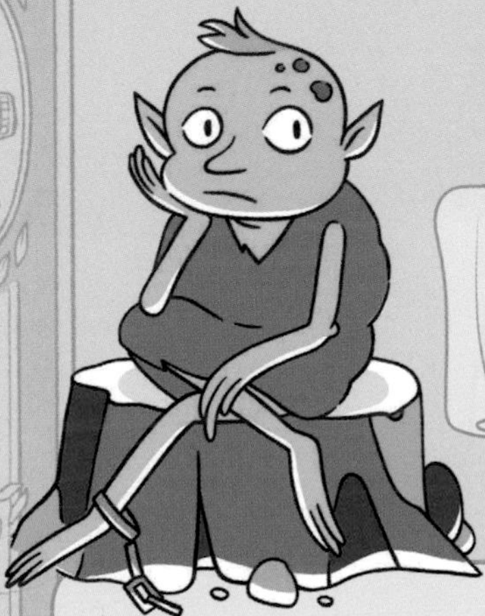

Persephone is known as the goddess of spring. When she emerges from the Underworld, spring begins.

Persephone has two children. One is a nymph who brings nightmares. The other is the god of the grape harvest. In some myths, she is also the mother of three sisters, who are the goddesses of vengeance.

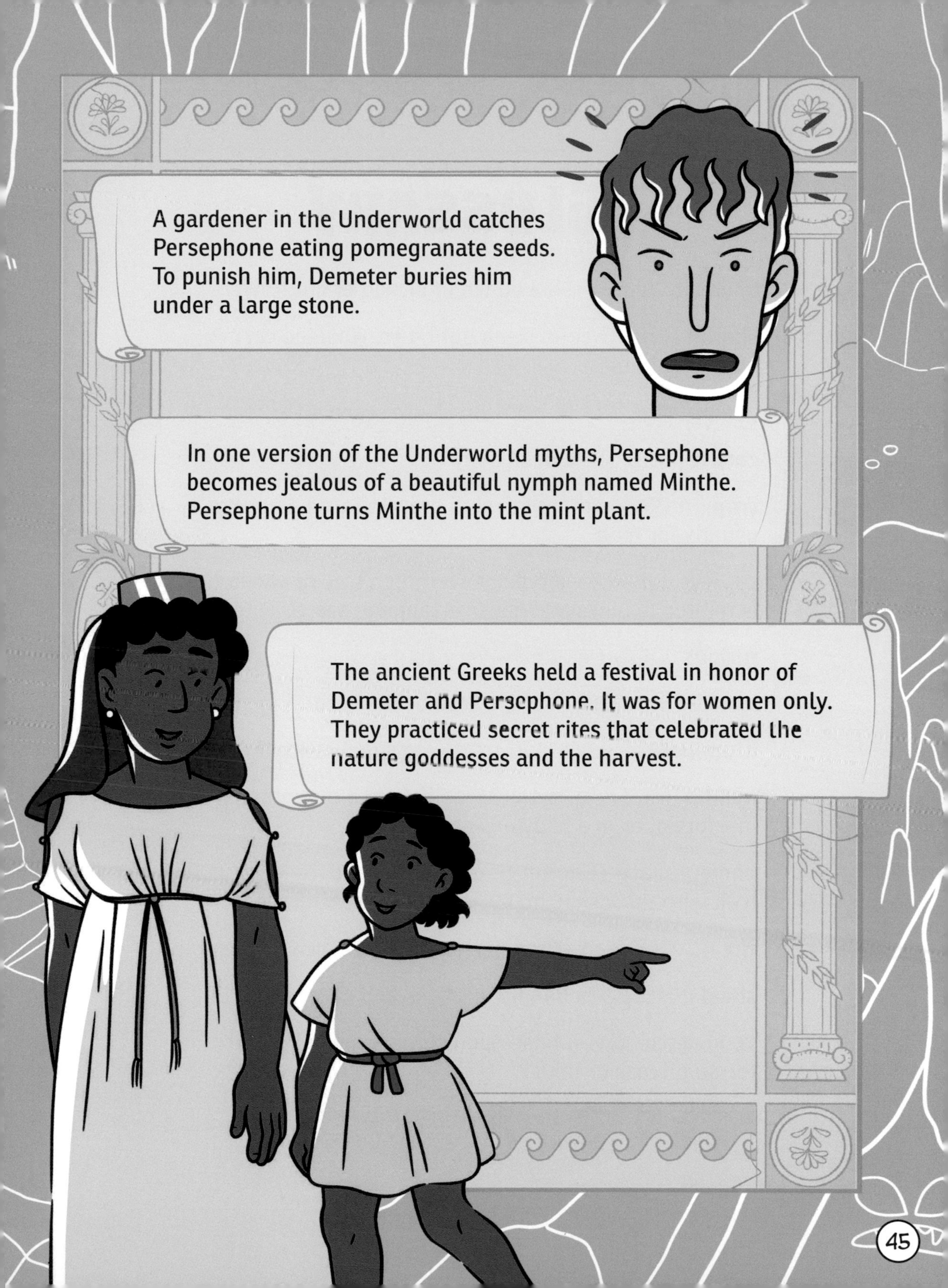
A gardener in the Underworld catches Persephone eating pomegranate seeds. To punish him, Demeter buries him under a large stone.
In one version of the Underworld myths, Persephone becomes jealous of a beautiful nymph named Minthe. Persephone turns Minthe into the mint plant.
The ancient Greeks held a festival in honor of Demeter and Persephone. It was for women only. They practiced secret rites that celebrated the nature goddesses and the harvest.

GLOSSARY

bouquet (boh-KAY)—a bunch of picked or cut flowers

chariot (CHAYR-ee-uht)—a light, two-wheeled cart pulled by horses

compromise (KAHM-pruh-myz)—to reach an agreement

corpse (KORPS)—a dead body

crop (KROP)—a plant farmers grow in large amounts, usually for food

cypress (SIP-ris)—a type of evergreen tree or shrub that is related to pines and has overlapping, scalelike leaves

furious (FYOOR-ee-uhs)—very angry

harvest (HAR-vist)—a ripe crop or the gathering of a crop

illuminate (ih-LOO-muh-neyt)—to supply with light

nymph (NIMF)—a mythical maiden on a mountain, in a forest, or in a body of water

pomegranate (POM-uh-gran-it)—a round, reddish-yellow fruit with thick skin, many seeds, and a tart flavor

rite (RAYHT)—an action performed as part of a ceremony

sheaf (SHEEF)—a bundle of stalks and ears of grain

vengeance (VEN-juhns)—punishment given in return for an offense or injury

Internet Sites

Britannica: Persephone
britannica.com/topic/Persephone-Greek-goddess

Ducksters: Greek Mythology: Hades
ducksters.com/history/ancient_greece/hades.php

Kiddle: Persephone Facts for Kids
kids.kiddle.co/Persephone

Other Books in This Series

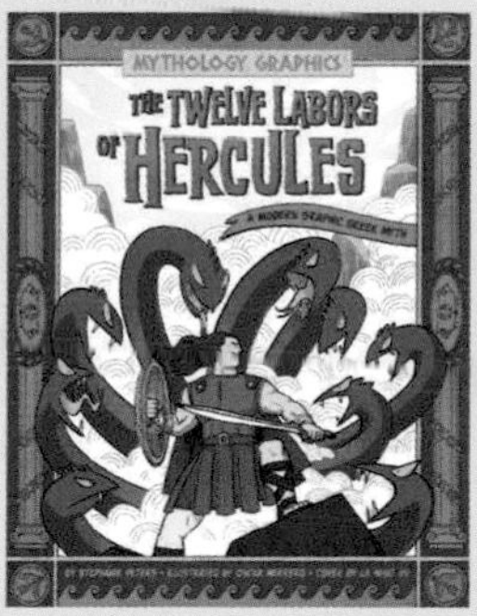
MYTHOLOGY GRAPHICS
THE TWELVE LABORS OF HERCULES

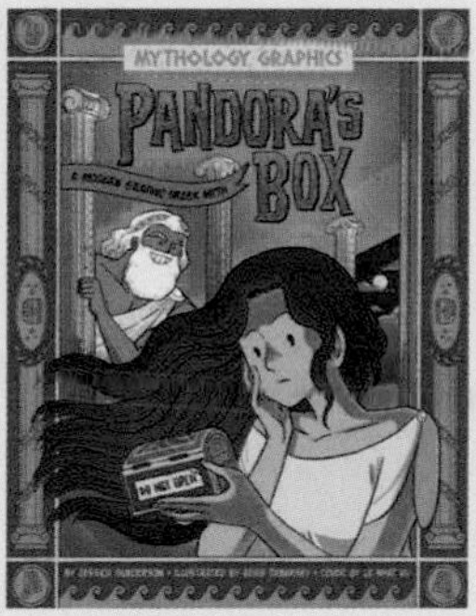
MYTHOLOGY GRAPHICS
PANDORA'S BOX

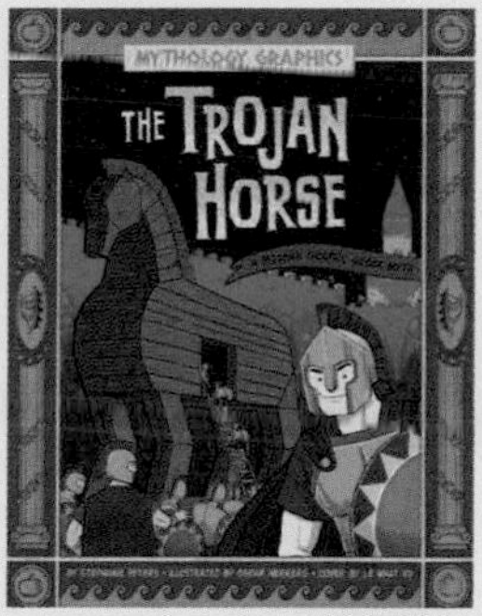
MYTHOLOGY GRAPHICS
THE TROJAN HORSE

About the Creators

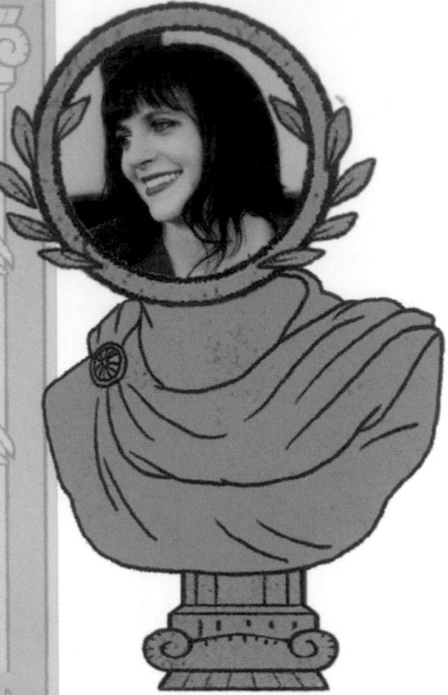

Jessica Gunderson grew up in the small town of Washburn, North Dakota. She has a bachelor's degree from the University of North Dakota and an MFA in Creative Writing from Minnesota State University, Mankato. She has written more than 75 books for young readers. Her book *President Lincoln's Killer and the America He Left Behind* won a 2018 Eureka! Nonfiction Children's Book Silver Award. She currently lives in Madison, Wisconsin.

Photo Credit: Anda Marie Photography

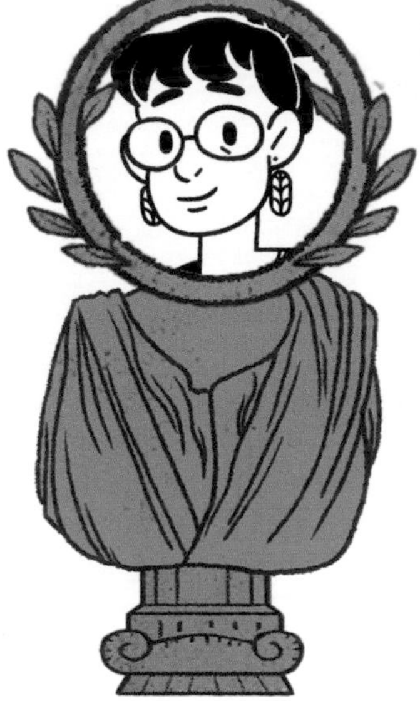

Jessi Zabarsky is a cartoonist and illustrator living in Chicago, Illinois. She makes comics about girls, magic, big feelings, and fantastic worlds. Her first two graphic novels, *Witchlight* and *Coming Back*, are available from Random House Graphic. She has stopped counting her houseplants, as there are now far too many.

Image Credit: Jessi Zabarsky

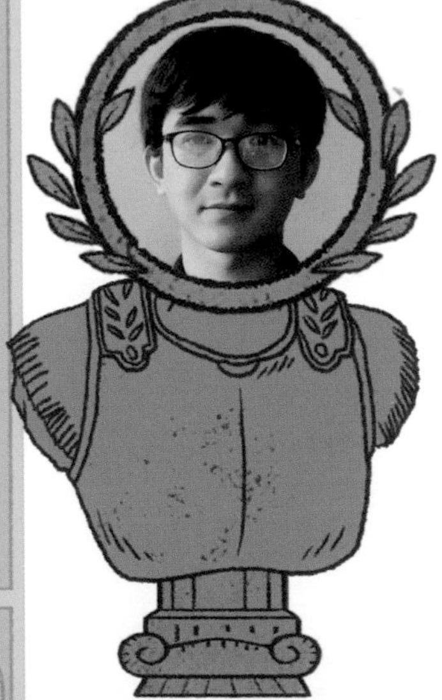

Le Nhat Vu was born in Nha Trang, a seaside city in Vietnam. He now works as a book illustrator in Ho Chi Minh City. He draws inspiration from fantasy, adventure, and poetic stories. During his free time, he enjoys reading Japanese comics (manga) and novels as well as watching football and movies—maybe with a cup of milk coffee.

Photo Credit: Le Nhat Vu